A Cold Case

ACKNOWLEDGMENTS

FIRST THANKS GO to my cousin David Gourevitch, who introduced me to Andy Rosenzweig, and to Rosenzweig himself for telling me his story of the Frankie Koehler case and entrusting me to investigate it further. I give thanks also to the other men and women whose stories and voices make up this story, and I pay homage to the memory of Richie Glennon and Pete McGinn.

Many thanks to David Remnick for providing me with a home at *The New Yorker*, where portions of *A Cold Case* first appeared and where I am surrounded by colleagues who make work a pleasure. I am especially grateful for the enthusiastic dedication of my editor, Jeffrey Frank, for the good counsel of Henry Finder and Dorothy Wickenden, and for Bill Buford's steadfast generosity. Ben McGrath and Anne Stringfield in the fact-checking department, as well as Perri Dorset, Elizabeth Pearson-Griffiths, and Nicole LaPorte, all provided great help in this project.

Many thanks to Elisabeth Sifton, my editor at Farrar, Straus and Giroux, and to my publisher, Roger Straus, for their spirited commitment to my work. Many thanks for the long-standing support of Ursula Doyle, my editor at Picador-U.K. in London. Many thanks to Sarah Chalfant, my anchor at The Wylie Agency, a wise reader and kind friend, to Andrew Wylie, and to Michael Siegel of Michael Siegel and Associates.

And many special thanks for the generous hospitality of the Corporation of Yaddo, where much of this book was written.

Finally, I thank my parents, Jacqueline and Victor Gourevitch, my brother, Marc, and his family, and my friends Vijay Balakrishnan, Elizabeth Rubin, Gilles Peress, and Joey Xanders, whose companionship sustained me on the trail of *A Cold Case*.

PHILIP GOUREVITCH

A
Cold Case

Picador USA
Farrar, Straus and Giroux
New York

www.picadorusa.com

Picador® is a U.S. registered trademark and is used by Farrar, Straus and Giroux under license from Pan Books Limited.

For information on Picador USA Reading Group Guides, as well as ordering, please contact the Trade Marketing department at St. Martin's Press.
Phone: 1-800-221-7945 extension 763
Fax: 212-677-4456
E-mail: trademarketing@stmartins.com

Library of Congress Cataloging-in-Publication Data

Gourevitch, Philip.
    A cold case / by Philip Gourevitch.
       p. cm.
    ISBN 0-312-42002-1
    1. Koehler, Frank Gilbert. 2. Murder investigation—New York (State)—Case studies. I. Title.

HV6534.N5 G68 2001
364.15'23'097471—dc21   00-068179

First published in the United States by Farrar, Straus and Giroux

First Picador USA Edition: July 2002

10 9 8 7 6 5 4 3 2 1

for the girl

If the desire to kill and the opportunity to kill came always together, who would escape hanging?

—MARK TWAIN
PUDD'NHEAD WILSON'S NEW CALENDAR

CHAPTER ONE

ON NOVEMBER 15, 1944, an Army deserter named Frank
Gilbert Koehler was arrested for burglary in New York
City. Frankie, as he liked to be called, had no criminal
record. He had walked off his post at Fort Dix, New Jersey, after suffering unsustainable financial reversals in a
crap game in the latrine, and when it was discovered that
he was fifteen years old and had lied about his age to enlist, he was sent to children's court, declared a juvenile
delinquent, and returned to military control. Six months

later, Koehler—AWOL again, and for good—shot and killed a sixteen-year-old boy in an abandoned building on West Twenty-fourth Street. The next day, he surrendered to a policeman on a street corner and was taken to a station house, where he confessed. In consideration of his "extreme youth" and lack of "parental guidance"—he had left home at thirteen, following the death of his father, a burglar—the district attorney reduced his charge from homicide to murder in the second degree. In court, Koehler pleaded guilty, and the judge sent him upstate to spend five years at the Elmira Reformatory. He was released on May 17, 1950, and remained a free man for nine months and twenty-six days until he was found by police, at four in the morning, hiding on the catwalk between the tracks of the Third Avenue elevated train line at Thirty-fourth Street, after robbing a nearby bar and grill at gunpoint. As he was led back to the station platform, Koehler called out to a man standing there in the predawn gloom as if waiting for a train, "Arthur, save me, save me, tell them I was with you." So that man, too, was taken into custody. Koehler and he had indeed been together all night. They'd met at a Times Square cinema where the poster said THRILL CRAZY, KILL CRAZY, and the

4

PART ONE

Dead or Alive

picture was *Gun Crazy*, a story of fugitive lovers on a crime spree hurtling to their doom.

A news photograph of Koehler taken minutes after his arrest showed him to be a slight, dark-haired man, rather handsome and sharply dressed in an overcoat, business suit, white shirt, necktie, and handcuffs. When the picture appeared in the *Daily Mirror*, he was recognized by Carmella Basterrchea, the bookkeeper of a Murray Hill construction company, as one of two gunmen who had, a month earlier, stepped into her office late on a Friday afternoon, then, saying, "All right, lady, this is a heist," and, "Don't move or I'll plug you," made off with her payroll. Koehler admitted to both stickups, and once again he was sent upstate, this time to Green Haven Prison in Stormville, with a sentence of ten to twenty years. He served eleven and a half and was paroled in August 1962 at the age of thirty-three, having spent most of his life "away."

Before the year was out, Frankie Koehler had a wife and legitimate employment in a machine shop. Later, he found union work as a stevedore on the West Side docks, then on the crew at the New York Coliseum on Columbus Circle, and he did not come to the attention of the police

Frank Koehler, under arrest for armed robbery, March 1951.
Photograph from the Daily Mirror

again until February 18, 1970. Around eight o'clock on that evening, he was having drinks at Channel Seven, a restaurant on West Fifty-fourth Street, when he got into an argument with the owner, Pete McGinn, and a friend of McGinn's named Richie Glennon. The issue was a woman—the wife of a mutual friend. Koehler had been having an affair with her while her husband was in prison, and she was now pregnant. McGinn declared that knocking up a jailed friend's wife was about the lowest thing a lowlife could do, and Glennon seconded this judgment. Koehler came back with the opinion that they were a couple of scumbags themselves. So it went. Koehler spit in McGinn's face, and the three men were soon out on the sidewalk, where Glennon watched as McGinn and Koehler had at each other and Koehler took a severe beating.

After that, McGinn went home, Glennon returned to the bar, and Koehler picked himself up off the pavement and went his own way for a while before returning to Channel Seven. Glennon was still there. Koehler had a drink with him and proposed that they sit down with McGinn to put their quarrel behind them in a gentlemanly fashion. Glennon agreed, and phoned McGinn to say they were coming over to his place, which was a block north of Channel Seven, in what the next day's *News* described as a "luxury apartment building . . . just up the street from Gov. Rockefeller's New York office."

Richie Glennon and Pete McGinn had known each other from boyhood in the South Bronx, and both had found success in the restaurant business. McGinn's Channel Seven was a popular watering hole for disc jockeys and anchormen from the nearby studios of ABC television and CBS radio, and Glennon owned a bistro on the Upper East Side called The Flower Pot, which was doing well enough for him to have taken the night off. Glennon had been having dinner at Channel Seven with his girlfriend, a nurse, and when he left with Frankie Koehler, she accompanied them. "We went to McGinn's apartment, and rode up in the elevator," she told me nearly thirty years later. "It was the fourth floor. Richie told me to stay in the hall, and I waited out there till I heard these loud bangs. I thought they were fighting again, throwing things around. I heard the noise—I didn't even know they were shots, I just heard bangs—and I opened the door. Frankie Koehler was running away with his smoking gun. I said, 'Where's Richie?' There was Richie on the floor."

Glennon lay on his back with his legs crossed comfortably at his ankles, his overcoat and suit jacket twisted beneath him, his left arm flung out, and the left side of his shirt bunched and soaked in blood from shoulder to waist around a small round hole over his rib cage. His girlfriend didn't notice that Pete McGinn was at the far end of the room, clad only in a bathrobe, with his right foot in a slipper and his left foot bare, lying facedown and dead in a puddle of blood on the parquet floor. "I remember a big dog hopping around," she told me. "It wasn't a small dog. It was a big dog." Beyond that, she was conscious only of Glennon. She didn't want to believe he was dead. She tried to pick him up and ask him where it hurt.

Koehler told her to shut up. He was still hovering over her with his gun, and it occurred to her that he must be afraid. She said, "I'm not gonna tell anybody," and he said, "Don't open your fucking mouth. Just sit there." With that, he left. He took the elevator down to the lobby, fished a handkerchief from his pocket, and pretended to be coughing into it to hide his face as he walked past the doorman. And then Frankie Koehler disappeared.

CHAPTER TWO

TWENTY-SEVEN YEARS LATER, on January 6, 1997, Andy Rosenzweig, the chief of investigations for the district attorney of Manhattan, was driving up First Avenue, nosing through lunch hour traffic, on his way to New York Hospital for a stress test. The procedure was routine, one of the mounting burdens of middle age, but Rosenzweig had plenty to be stressed about—on any given day, his squad of more than eighty investigators was at work on hundreds of cases, tracking thousands of leads into virtually every known realm of criminal activity—and at the corner of Sixty-ninth Street, he experienced a jolt of memory that quickened his pulse. That was where Richie Glennon's restaurant, The Flower Pot, had stood. Rosenzweig, who had known Glennon and liked him, was vexed to realize that he couldn't say when he'd last recalled his murdered pal.

Rosenzweig didn't like to think of himself as a forgetful man; in his view of human qualities, forgetfulness ranked as a fundamental flaw. He could live with such failings in others. He had to. But with himself, he was less forgiving, and as the memory of Glennon revived in him, he went to work on it, tracking it back to the early 1960s, when he'd graduated from the prestigious Bronx High School of Science and, having no plan—no idea, really, of what to make of himself—he'd found work for several summers as a lifeguard at the Miramar pool at 207th Street and Tenth Avenue. It was the largest outdoor swimming pool in Manhattan, half a million gallons of water, with a high spiraling slide, and a terrace of deep sand called "the beach," and a cafeteria, and a former dance hall that served as a weight gym for the inside crowd. Glennon, a lanky, rugged-looking, blue-eyed former prizefighter became a regular on the Miramar scene in the summer of 1964, Rosenzweig's third season there. Glennon was ten years older than Rosenzweig, and when he first appeared at the pool, he pretended to be someone else, introducing himself around as a champion boxer of the day. He didn't fool anyone for long, but he made an impression. That was Glennon: through the deception, he had made himself known—always a kidder, always coming on as a big shot, always putting one over, an impersonator, always on the move. His hands in particular were never idle, flickering about to the syncopated rhythms of his speech, striking a range of distracting poses.

Yes, he boxed, but Glennon was no champion. In the ring, as a middleweight, he had a mediocre record, thirteen fights, five losses; he was what they called "a ham-and-egger." But just getting in there gave him an aura that he considered worth the beatings. He enjoyed fighting, and did it for free when the occasion presented itself in bars and on the street. He liked to mix things up. He liked to hang out with cops, and he liked to hang out with criminals—liked to be where the action was. He'd served in the merchant marine and worked as a model, and by the time Rosenzweig met him he was earning high union wages as an ironworker, fitting the frames of tall buildings. On the job, he'd hang a sign off the beam with his name and phone number and wave at the girls in the facing offices. And it worked; they'd call him. Rosenzweig, who tended to be as reserved as Glennon was antic, remembered him as a man of mischief, "a colorful character, high energy, funny, a talker, glib, Runyonesque—you know, a tough guy."

To be sure, Rosenzweig had always sensed "something behind the scenes with Richie," a whiff of the illicit. Glennon, he recalled, "was one of those pure New York characters who truly walked the fence between the good guys and the bad guys." At the same time, Rosenzweig had recognized in him a familiar hunger to be "somebody" without quite knowing who. In those days, Rosenzweig couldn't have said how his own qualities were supposed to add up, either. Back home, in the leafy, predominantly Jewish neighborhood of Bronx Park East, his father, a Polish-born cabdriver, and his mother, a Brooklyn-born professional secretary, wanted him to go to college. (After all, his mother told his friends, he had an IQ of 158.) But Rosenzweig was restless; classrooms oppressed him; his mind resisted abstraction, and he felt most at ease among the older, streetwise cops and construction workers who made up the core of his crowd at the Miramar.

His boss at the pool was an Irish Catholic ex-cop named Danny Lynch, who was in his mid-thirties and claimed he'd never met a Jew before and had never wanted to. "Rosen-what?" people at the pool would say when they heard his name. "How do you spell that?" Rosenzweig would answer them, and Lynch would chant the letters to the tune of the Mouseketeers: R-O-S, E-N-Z, W-E-I-G. Lynch was impressed by anyone agile enough to avoid taking the bait without backing down, and during Rosenzweig's second summer at the Miramar, they became best friends. "He was up for us," Lynch recalled. "You couldn't intimidate Andy, physically or mentally." Lynch was no slouch himself. In 1956, as a twenty-one-year-old police rookie just back from military service in Korea, he was made a detective—the youngest ever in the city—after displaying extraordinary reflexes under extraordinary pressure. He told me of the incident, much as he had told it to young Andy Rosenzweig nearly half a century earlier.

"Michael Sudia, a big, tall, six-foot-four, beautiful-looking kid, same age as myself, and a little guy, Felix Durante, had the whole West Side terrorized, doing stick-ups. They were heroin addicts, and deserters from the Marine Corps, and they'd got in a shooting in the Hotel Whitehall on a Hundredth Street and Broadway. I didn't know it. I was standing down in Riverside Drive, a new cop, on what they call a fixer. That's a fixed post. You have to stand there. This was December, a cold December night, and for some reason they decided to run toward me. I could hear them running down the street. There was no one else around from West End Avenue to the Drive, just a lot of doctors' cars. I figured they'd broke into a car, no big deal. So when they got abreast of me, I stepped out and had my arms out with my nightstick. Sudia put a pistol to my head and said, 'You cocksucker, hand me your gun, or I'll kill you.' So—I'm not sure of the exchange, but I'm pretty sure—I said, 'OK, OK.' And I went into my coat. We had big heavy coats that you're too young to have seen. They wrapped around you, terrible heavy coats. If you could stand up in them all night, you were lucky to walk home. Anyway, when I cleared the holster, I fired through my coat. I shot him six times. You know how many times I hit him? Twice. Once in the heart—he had a tattoo of a heart on his heart—once in the knee. The others passed through his clothing, and our noses were touching, so I guess I was frightened. He was dead by the time his head was by my knees."

Days at the Miramar were a run of such stories, and there were always more cops to be found around the corner at Chambers' bar, where Rosenzweig soon became an after-work regular. Richie Glennon was never at the center of that life, but he made himself at home in it. There was a time when Rosenzweig wanted to get into ironwork, and Glennon sent him down to meet the boss at the union hall. But Jews were not wanted. The boss said, " 'Rosenzweig' is not gonna fly around here. Will you use another name?" and Rosenzweig said, "No."

Later, when Rosenzweig followed Lynch's urgings and became a cop and Glennon moved into the restaurant business, they had faded to the periphery of each other's worlds, because Rosenzweig was rigorously straight and Glennon remained a man of many hustles who "never quite separated himself from the underbelly of life" and was known as a "shylock," a loan shark. Still, when Rosenzweig got married in 1967, Glennon attended the wedding, and when Glennon got shot in 1970, Rosenzweig attended his wake. Rosenzweig had seen a good deal of violent death by then, working as a patrolman in the Four-One Precinct—"Fort Apache"—in the Bronx. But Glennon was the first person he had known socially to be murdered, and nothing he'd learned on the job helped to diminish the shock when Danny Lynch called him with the news.

Passing the site of the old Flower Pot brought it all back: Glennon and McGinn—double homicide. It was the talk of Rosenzweig's town at the time, and a curious thing about murder is the way it twists one's memory of the dead into a fixation on the murderer. "Everyone knew this guy Frankie Koehler had shot and killed Richie and Pete," Rosenzweig recalled. "It was like a simple case. It wasn't a whodunit, just, Where is he? It was kind of matter-of-fact. People saying, 'Oh, yeah, they just gotta pick him up. They know where he lives, they know he works at the Coliseum. Frankie Koehler, bad guy, tough guy, West Side of Manhattan, real bad guy.' It was almost like a fait accompli: 'They're gonna find him because detectives do that. They know how to do it.' Every day and every week, and then every few weeks and then every few months, we'd talk about it: 'Aw, jeez, they still have to pick him up.' Maybe a year went by and they didn't pick him up, maybe two years, and you're moving on in life."

TWENTY-SEVEN YEARS. The Miramar pool had been paved over long ago, and a Pathmark supermarket now stood in its place. Somewhere Rosenzweig still had a photograph of himself with Danny Lynch and some of their long-ago crowd gathered around a table at a policeman's retirement banquet in the late 1960s: ten flashbulb-bright faces, all of them cops with their wives and dates, except for Richie Glennon and his girlfriend. Half the people at that table were dead now. "Their peephole is closed," Rosenzweig told me. He himself was fifty-two; his three children were grown; he had recently married his third wife, Mary Kelley, who worked with him at the D.A.'s office as the master of computer searches; they had just bought a weekend house together on the Rhode Island shore; and as he was beginning, warily, to contemplate retirement, he looked back to the time when he had known Glennon as "the formative years," and he felt a sense of debt. He figured that if Koehler had ever been caught, he would have heard, and as an officer of the law, he took the fact that he hadn't heard as a rebuke.

There is no statute of limitations on murder. Although a case may turn cold, the hunt for a killer remains officially open until he is captured and convicted or until he is dead, and although New York has an 87 percent closure rate for murder cases (almost 20 percent above the national average), Rosenzweig believed that murdered people and their survivors deserved even better statistics. He had always admired homicide detectives, who "handled death on a routine basis." But he also knew what it meant to police the city—he had been recognized early on as an "active cop," and as his record of solid and increasingly sophisticated arrests stacked up, he had been made a sergeant at twenty-eight and a lieutenant at thirty-five—and he said, "The system doesn't always work so well."

Rosenzweig is an understated man in the implacable manner of Humphrey Bogart, to whom he bears some resemblance: he has the trim proportions, though he is more muscular; he has the versatile, long, toothy face, at once bemused and brooding, with a smile that bares a hint of a snarl and a sense of preoccupation with his own private calculus; and his nasal, slightly sibilant speech recalls Bogart's nervous rhythms. When I asked him if it was true, as I'd heard, that he once grabbed the Mafia godfather John Gotti on a street in Little Italy and threw him against a wall, he said, "There was such an incident." Then, after a minute, he said, "I threw a lot of people against walls." I could imagine. His hands are large, with fingers that are thick at the base and taper to a surprising fineness.

I first met Rosenzweig in the spring of 1999, at the D.A.'s office, where he directed me onto a green leather couch and sat himself on a little metal folding chair with his brown suit trousers riding up his shins. On his left ankle was strapped a black Velcro holster with a .380 eight-shot automatic, and as he described how the memory of Richie Glennon's murder came to him on the way to his medical checkup he told me that Glennon's girlfriend had never married, and McGinn had been survived by a wife and four young children, who lived in the suburbs. Rosenzweig remembered driving up First Avenue, thinking of how a homicide detective he knew used to say: "Who speaks for the dead? Nobody. As a rule, nobody speaks for the dead, unless we do."

Rosenzweig wasn't too happy with his stress test that day. The doctors gave him a clean bill of health, but he knew the drill, and it irked him that nobody had taken the trouble to start him out on a treadmill. "They just had me lie on the table, and hooked me up with wires," he said, "which doesn't necessarily detect the anomalies that you want to detect." Rosenzweig, whose life's work consisted in detecting anomalies, didn't protest, "in order not to cause any more stress," but he left the hospital feeling sloppily treated, and as soon as he got to a phone, he called Danny Lynch to ask, "Did they ever get that guy Frankie Koehler?"

Lynch didn't know. He reminded Rosenzweig that he'd been at Channel Seven himself, having a drink with Glennon and McGinn, on the evening they were killed, and he sounded chagrined to be reminded that he, too, had lost track of the case.

"You're the D.A.'s chief investigator," Lynch said. "And you're asking me?"

Rosenzweig said, "Good point."

That afternoon, he opened a blank notebook and wrote Frankie Koehler's name on the first page; he made a few more calls, and before long, he had jotted down a piece of information: "Two tattoos on left arm—a skull and crossbones and a heart." A few days later, he sent a man from his homicide unit up to the Midtown North station house to collect the old files on Koehler. The sergeant there knew Rosenzweig, and he said, "Hey, ask Andy why he's looking at this. This case is closed. This guy's dead."

CHAPTER THREE

DETECTIVES DO A LOT OF WRITING, and one of the most frequently used phrases in their professional prose is "negative results." After all, the great part of a detective's working life is spent following seemingly fruitless leads, then writing about what was done, seen, and heard along the way on a "Complaint Follow Up" form, known in New York as a D-D-Five. Each new D-D-Five is filed away atop all the previous D-D-Fives for a given investigation, and, sure enough, when Andy Rosenzweig opened

the file on the Glennon-McGinn double homicide, the top
D-D-Five, written in May 1992, bore the heading "Basis
for Closing Case with Exceptional Clearance," and the
first sentence said, "After an extensive investigation by
the undersigned and other Detectives over a period of
twenty-two years it is the opinion of the undersigned that
the subject Frank G. Koehler is dead."

The word that snagged Rosenzweig's eye was "opinion." By law, homicide cases can be closed with Exceptional Clearance only when the subject's death is a matter
of fact substantiated by fingerprints from the corpse, a
death certificate, or an obituary. The detective who closed
the Koehler case had none of these. His conclusion was
based entirely on negative results: "The subject has not
surfaced . . . which leads one to reasonably believe that
the subject is dead." In fact, the detective argued, those
who knew Koehler best considered it virtually inconceiv-
able that a man with such a violent disposition and criminal history could have remained alive and out of trouble
for more than twenty years.

Strikingly, most of the people who had advanced this
notion to the detective were Koehler's relatives—and

even they left some doubt. Koehler's seventy-nine-year-old mother, for instance, who was found at the Blue Angel Motel in Las Vegas, said that she had heard in the early 1970s that Frankie had been shot and killed, but then she said that she had later been told he was living in Boston. The detective had asked her to submit to a polygraph test, but she had refused. And the manager of the Blue Angel, one Eula Chesser, told the detective that Koehler's mother had spoken of Frankie's existence in conditional terms, saying, "If he were alive, the police would never take him alive, in that he had a bad temper." The detective had also contacted a niece of Koehler's in Chula Vista, California, who struck a similarly cryptic note, saying she'd stopped asking about her vanished uncle four years earlier, in 1988, when she'd spoken about Koehler with his only brother, Kenny, and was told, "When you live by the gun, you die by the gun." Yet when Kenny himself met with the detective at a coffee shop called the Top and Top in Queens, he said he was sure he would have heard if his brother had died. Kenny, who had also worked at the New York Coliseum, allowed that Frankie was a rough customer, but he said he'd had no news of the fugitive since the night of the murders, at which time, he claimed, "Frank went to the Coliseum and robbed a shylock in order to get money to get out of town." When the detective pushed harder, asking how Frankie Koehler could have survived without running into the law for twenty years, Kenny replied, "Maybe if he completely changed his environment."

"I don't fucking believe this," Rosenzweig remembers saying as he read the detective's report. "There's nothing in here to conclude he's dead other than that his mother and his brother said, 'Frank was a bad boy.' " The detective who had closed the case had a good reputation, and Rosenzweig suspected that he had given up and declared Koehler dead only under pressure from his superiors. "That's clearance on two homicides," he explained, adding, "It's a particular squad lieutenant's advantage to have a high closure rate. Some of them do it legit, and some of them cut corners." Such was the nature of the system, he said: a low-profile case could slip through the cracks, and it was "no individual's fault."

Rosenzweig is an avid reader, with a taste for European police procedurals, and he once read me a passage that rang especially true to him from *Smilla's Sense of Snow* by the Danish novelist Peter Høeg. In it, a man named Ravn, who works at the D.A.'s office in Copenhagen, speaks of his colleagues—detectives, investigators, and prosecutors—saying, "We were the suspicious ones. We believed that a statement, a confession, an incident, was seldom what it purported to be." At the same time, Ravn says, the fundamental requirement for a career in the Ministry of Justice is institutional loyalty, which means never turning "the excellent tool" of one's suspicion on the system itself. And, he concludes, "I can tell you that most people secretly find it a relief to have the state divest them of the trouble of being an independent person."

Rosenzweig had never known such relief. Throughout his career, he had striven to work for the system by working against the downward tug of its averages. Now, as he brooded on the manner in which the hunt for Frankie Koehler had been abandoned, it seemed to him that he held in his hands—in a single fat file stuffed with documents telling of one man's disappearance—a mystery that contained in the most personal way his own struggles and exasperations with that system which he wanted fiercely to believe in but which kept undermining and testing his faith.

THE FOUR-ONE PRECINCT, when Rosenzweig started out as a patrolman there, had one of the highest crime rates in the world. "A fun place to work," he said. But he quickly found that many of his colleagues thought it was more fun to let the criminals work for them. The New York City Police Department back then was what he politely called "interesting"—rife with men who regarded the badge more as a license to corruption than as a bond to public service and who took as their motto the infamous quip attributed to former mayor William O'Dwyer: "A cop who doesn't know how to make a buck out there shouldn't be a cop." It wasn't as if everyone in the Four-One station house was on the take, but Rosenzweig, whose after-tax pay came to ninety-five dollars a week, heard officers boasting that they collected as much as a thousand dirty dollars a month and that they never spent unpaid overtime hours in court because they hardly ever arrested anyone.

"I went out with a guy, Eddie, a monster for traffic shakedowns," he said. "He had a fine schedule, and set goals, a hundred dollars a shift. He says to me, 'You owe it to yourself. You got a family.' " Rosenzweig asked for a new partner, and he got one. This cop, an older guy, drove straight to a dark, cave-like spot under a highway over-pass along the Sheridan Expressway, parked there in high weeds, and said, "You want the back seat or front?" Rosenzweig said he wasn't getting in back. "Well, don't answer the radio," the man said, then went to the trunk, returned with a pillow and a blanket, and proceeded to take off his shoes, his gun belt, and his pants. "In those days," Rosenzweig told me, "a lot of cops cooped, mean-ing they napped a lot. They had a wonderful facility, or faculty, for being able to find a place to hide in a very ur-ban area. It was kind of accepted practice, winked at by supervisors—some of them did it themselves. And my heart would go out to the radio dispatchers, who would be looking for a unit to answer a call because people were waiting for help to come." That night, in the weeds, while his partner slept, Rosenzweig listened to the voice on the radio working alphabetically through the precinct's call signals, searching for a car to go to a reported burglary in progress. When he heard his handle, Four-One-Mike, he said, "Whaddya got, Central?" He had the car in gear be-

Andy Rosenzweig as a young patrolman

fore his partner woke up, growling as he pulled on his pants, "What are you—crazy? You stupid bastard." Rosenzweig told him, "Listen, fuck you."

"You didn't have to have a lot of experiences like that," Rosenzweig said, "because people got to know you pretty well, and you got the reputation: He's a pain in the ass, a hardnose." He quickly identified the active cops in the precinct and turned to them as teachers, asking, "How do you know what to look for? How do you know gambling or narcotics? How do you know what a stickup man looks like? What do you look for when you come upon a burglary, which is a very hard case to solve once it's happened? What do you look for? How do you look for it? How do you make an observation?" Policing New York in the late 1960s was still intimate work, conducted largely on foot, by eye, and by ear, and Rosenzweig believed that was how it should be. "When I started out, they didn't have walkie-talkies," he said. "You had to become a part of the neighborhood so people would talk to you and tell you things." Later, he had opposed the introduction of air-conditioned police cars, arguing, quixotically, that it was the practical equivalent of allowing cops to coop while awake. "You can't hear people," he said. "You're so removed from reality."

Such avidity, along with his penchant for arresting the same bookmakers and dope dealers from whom his colleagues collected protection money, sometimes made Rosenzweig's life lonely at the station house. But he took courage from the advice given him when he entered

the police academy by a crusty old cop at Chambers'
bar named Jack "One Punch" Minogue: "You're comin'
on the job? Let me tell you something, kid. Don't listen
to the bullshitters. Do the extra work. Answer the extra
calls. Go the extra yard. It'll pay off in the long run." To
a less susceptible ear Minogue's speech might have
sounded like the white noise of clichés, but Rosenzweig
heard in it an animating challenge, and he made it his
mantra. After all, he said, "Everything we do, there's a
victim attached."

ROSENZWEIG COULDN'T REMEMBER the first time he was
called to a murder in the Four-One, but one early scene
stood out for him. "Dope people," he said. "Guy shot his
girlfriend in the head, then shot himself in the head." He
was filling in for an absentee that day, and when the call
came for an "aided case"—an injured or sick person—
his temporary partner wanted time to finish his coffee.
"Sometimes I don't even go on these things," he said.
Rosenzweig said, "I think we better go." His partner
called him a "ball buster" and began driving—"in not
too much of a hurry," Rosenzweig recalled. When they finally arrived, the murderer-suicide was still alive, though

barely, and while Rosenzweig kicked the gun away from the man's hand and set about securing the scene, his partner just stood there and watched. Later, Rosenzweig's sergeant complimented him. "Nice for a young cop," Rosenzweig said, but in telling me such stories, he wasn't really bragging. He was saying that too often, in his work experience, doing things right amounted to little more than refusing to do things wrong.

"Right is right," he liked to say. He couldn't be called a romantic, because he despised self-deception, yet there was an undeniable romance in his sense of vocation; he loved being a cop and an investigator—loved the work itself as much as its purpose. Still, he remained embarrassed and offended by the system's capacity to accommodate the common run of what, on a forgiving day, he would call nitwits: not so much those who can't do any better, but those who can't be bothered.

So it angered Rosenzweig to think that Frankie Koehler might have been granted the fugitive's ultimate sanctuary of official death. In the D.A.'s office hierarchy, he wasn't authorized to open an investigation without the backing of a prosecutor, but he didn't want to have to explain himself. He decided not to discuss the Koehler case with anybody in the office except his wife, Mary, and he asked her to search her computer databases—death files, Social Security numbers, press archives—for any indication that Koehler had died. When she came back with negative results, he flipped the old case files over and started digging through them from the beginning. "I don't like to leave things hanging," he told me, "and I thought it might make it a little less hard to retire if I got this thing settled."

CHAPTER FOUR

ROSENZWEIG TENDED TO ENJOY his work most when he was out of the office, exercising his considerable powers as a noticer: looking for trouble, tracking leads, questioning sources, and—if all the pieces added up—catching criminals. But he didn't mind sitting behind a desk when an investigation was at stake. In his experience, paperwork and legwork frequently went hand in hand. In 1974, while stuck in traffic on a service road of the Major Deegan Expressway in the South Bronx, he had watched a man in a new yellow Cadillac pull over and park on the sidewalk. Rosenzweig was off duty (on vacation, actually), but he couldn't help registering that this was an odd place to park. When the man got out of his car—"kind of duded up, and carrying a little paper bag"—Rosenzweig, whose interest in the drug trade made him prone to excitement at the sight of little paper bags, began having a conversation with himself:

"Mind your own business. You're on vacation."

"Yeah, but if he crosses over the Major Deegan, there's something wrong. Why would he park here and walk over the bridge?"

The man crossed the bridge, and Rosenzweig followed him. "I didn't turn the steering wheel—it just turned," he said, as if he were merely a servant of his own suspicion. The man kept walking and Rosenzweig cruised slowly behind him, growing surer in his conviction, with each passing block, that the bag contained contraband. But he had no evidence, and he didn't have all day to do surveillance, so he pulled ahead, cut a U-turn, got out, and stood on the sidewalk. The man wouldn't make eye contact.

"He walks by and he's whistling," Rosenzweig said,

"but he's not whistling any tune. I get behind him, and I get ready. When he turns around I'm gonna give him the motion. The motion is just the badge in the hand. I know he's gonna turn, and he does, and I nod at the badge, and he takes off—big chase, on foot, cars screeching, we're going over hoods, I had my gun out." Rosenzweig finally caught the man ducking into a luncheonette. "I'm just going in here for a sandwich," the man said. But his paper bag contained at least eight ounces of cocaine.

A few days later, when Rosenzweig got hold of the suspect's rap sheet, he again fixed on something peculiar: the man had been arrested twice before in New York, and it appeared that earlier in his life he had been sent to prison in South Carolina with a life sentence. Rosenzweig didn't want to believe that nobody involved with the man's past New York arrests had noticed he might be an escaped convict, but he called South Carolina. "Rosen-*what*?" the sheriff's deputy said; then, when he heard the suspect's name, "Yup, we're looking for that boy."

Legwork, paperwork: that had been the end of one man's life in the outside world, and now, as Rosenzweig turned his attention to Frankie Koehler, he once more began noticing loose threads that quickened his interest.

For instance, there was a D-D-Five written in June of 1984 by a detective who had made a run out to Queens to visit the manager of the apartment building where Kenny Koehler had lived until a few years before. The detective showed the manager a photograph of Frankie taken at Green Haven Prison when he was paroled in 1962, and the manager recognized him, remarking that Frankie used to visit his brother at least twice a week and his appearance had hardly changed. Rosenzweig also came across other hints that Koehler had continued to frequent if not to live in New York long after the murders, and he was particularly intrigued by suggestions that Koehler had kept on working from time to time at the Coliseum.

Throughout the 1960s and well into the 1970s, the unions at the Coliseum had been controlled by competing criminal syndicates—notably the Hell's Kitchen Irish mob and the Gambino and Genovese Mafia families— and the D.A.'s office had conducted a number of investigations of racketeering there. In fact, the old membership rolls from Koehler's union, Local 829 of the International Alliance of Theatrical Stage Employees, were still in the office files, and Rosenzweig decided to look them over. He didn't expect much, and searching through the hundreds of names, Social Security and union-card numbers, and addresses, he found no trace of the murderer. But as he worked his way down the columns of birth dates, he got interested in a man named Frank Fitzgerald, who was registered as having been born on August 25, 1930—exactly a year, a month, and a day after Koehler himself.

Plus one, plus one, plus one: Rosenzweig knew that criminals frequently used such simple mnemonic devices when constructing aliases, and they often retained their first names too. What's more, Fitzgerald's address was in Toms River, New Jersey, which corresponded to another trace in the Koehler file: in August 1972, an informer told a detective on the case that Koehler was living on the Jersey shore and had been seen in the past month at a men's hotel called the Berkshire in Keansburg. That tip had produced the usual negative results, but the Jersey connection encouraged Rosenzweig to ask his wife to find out what her computer could tell them about Frank Fitzgerald. She reported back that he had no criminal record, but he did have a driver's license, which said that his eyes, like Koehler's, were blue and his height, like Koehler's, was five nine.

When Rosenzweig saw the ID photo from Fitzgerald's

license, he was astonished by the man's resemblance to Koehler. But Mary wasn't convinced, and Rosenzweig feared that his eagerness for Frank Fitzgerald to be Frankie Koehler could be prejudicing his vision. After all, he had only two pictures of Koehler: his Green Haven parole portrait, which was thirty-five years old; and an image produced in 1990 by an FBI computer-animation program, in which the parole photograph had been "aged" to represent a grayed and timeworn version of the fugitive. He decided to ask a handful of sharp-eyed col- leagues what they thought of the Fitzgerald and Koehler pictures. He didn't say who was who or why he cared, but everyone he consulted said the likeness was striking. Rosenzweig's response was: "Let's go get him. Cut to the chase."

CHAPTER FIVE

WHEN DETECTIVES SPEAK of the moment that a crime becomes theirs to investigate, they speak of "catching a case," and once caught, a case is like a cold: it clouds and consumes the catcher's mind until, like a fever, it breaks; or, if it remains unsolved, it is passed on like a contagion, from one detective to another, without ever entirely releasing its hold on those who catch it along the way. In New York, on every shift, every detective squad has its designated catchers, and on the night of Wednesday, February 18, 1970, Tom Hallinan had been catching for the Eighteenth squad in midtown when the call "Shots fired" went out over the radio, followed by Pete McGinn's address. Hallinan happened to be just a block away at the time, on his way to investigate a burglary, and he reached McGinn's apartment less than ten minutes after Koehler had left. The smell of gunpowder and smoke reminded him of the police firing range. "And on the floor," he said, "was the terrible sight."

Hallinan is a tall man with the sort of ruddy, smooth-worn slope of a face that Irish Americans are wont to describe, in a spirit of tribal affection, as looking like the map of Ireland. His hair is now white; his eyes, which are blue, appear at once pale and bright; and just off the tail of his left eyebrow, his skin is furrowed around a vertical scar. "I was stabbed in '69—very deep," he told me, and he described how he'd tried to stop a man on the street, felt the blade enter his head, then fallen to the sidewalk, blinded by blood and "thinking of Kennedy" as he groped for his gun. "The things you run across," he said, and he wasn't complaining. In 1986, Hallinan retired from the force as a sergeant in charge of detectives, and he now serves as director of corporate security for the

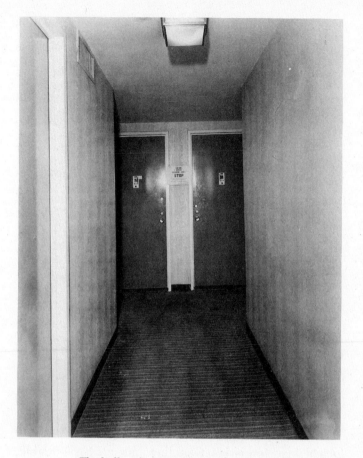

The hallway to Pete McGinn's apartment

telephone company Verizon, where the walls and shelves of his office are decked with plaques and photos from his life as a cop—twenty-four years, during which he received every major award the New York City Police Department can bestow on its officers except the medal of honor. "A great career," he told me. "Everything was positive. The only negative event was not apprehending Frankie Koehler."

So when Andy Rosenzweig called him from the D.A.'s office in January 1997 and said, "Tom, I want to ask you about an old case of yours," Hallinan didn't have to ask which one. "Frankie Koehler," he said. "He's the only guy I never caught. My family still kids me about it—'When are you gonna catch that guy?' "

Hallinan had identified the murderer within five minutes. In a back room of McGinn's apartment, he and his colleagues found an older man bleeding from a bullet wound in his leg. This turned out to be McGinn's uncle Charlie, who worked as a maître d' at Channel Seven. He had witnessed his nephew's fight with Koehler earlier in the evening, and when Koehler returned to the bar, Charlie had come to warn McGinn that there could be trouble. Later, when he heard gunfire in the living room, he had stepped in, got shot, and dragged himself away to hide in

OPPOSITE *The bodies: Richie Glennon* (above) *and Pete McGinn* (below) *in McGinn's living room*

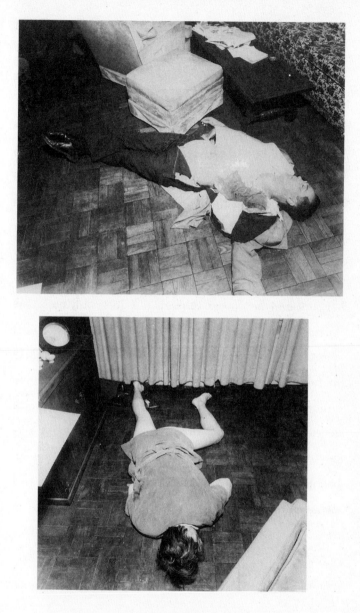

the bathroom. Hallinan called for an ambulance, and while he waited, he ran an address check on Koehler and dispatched a surveillance team to watch his apartment building in Queens. But Koehler had a twenty-minute head start, and, as Hallinan learned when he went to see Koehler's wife the next day, although he did go home after the killings, he had not lingered.

Mrs. Koehler said she'd been in all evening. She'd watched a show starring Anne Bancroft on television, and shortly after the eleven o'clock news came on (at about the same time that Hallinan first heard Koehler's name), her husband had come through the door with cuts and bruises on his face, saying, "Get out of my way. I had a fight. Don't bother me." In his anger, he then smashed the television set, and his wife, fearing a beating herself, withdrew to the kitchen while he washed his face, took some cash from the bedroom, and left. She said she didn't know where he could be. Hallinan stuck around for a while to see if she might become more cooperative, and she made him coffee, but that was all he got out of her.

So it went. As Hallinan and his colleagues interviewed and re-interviewed Koehler's relatives, friends, and acquaintances, watched their comings and goings from parked cars and shadowy doorways, and listened through headphones to their wiretapped phone calls, they swiftly assembled an excellent profile of the tangled relationships of his extended family and of his contacts in the criminal milieu of Manhattan's West Side: the rough-and-tumble, working-class neighborhoods of Chelsea and Hell's Kitchen that radiated out from the seedy core of Times Square to the mob-controlled Hudson River docks—a scramble of tenement blocks, sweatshops, freight yards, and warehouses, reaching south to the meatpacking district at Fourteenth Street and north along the all-night drug and sex markets that bordered the theater district. These were the streets where Koehler had grown up and to which he had always returned when he got out of jail, and he was well known and feared there by the young and brutal Irish racketeers, known as the Westies, who were making a name for themselves as master murderers and dismemberers.

Hallinan soon felt that he was getting to know more about the people in Koehler's life than many of them knew about one another, and he didn't doubt that if the pressure could be kept on them, the man himself would eventually be flushed out or ratted on. But in New York in

1970 the murder rate was twice what it is today—more than a thousand people were killed in the city that year—and after just several weeks of full-time work on Koehler, Hallinan and his partners were "right back in the squad, catching other cases."

Still, Hallinan said, "Koehler haunted us." He couldn't shake the nagging awareness that "there was something I had left undone," and when a criminal informant told him one day in the early 1970s of an address in Queens where he could find a hit man who had committed a double homicide, his first thought was, Sounds like Koehler. He and his partner, John Stein, decided to watch the man for a while, and, finding him to be a suspicious character—he always sent his girlfriend out of the house to look around and open his car before he followed and quickly drove away—they decided to grab him. So, Stein went out, found a stray dog, tied a piece of rope around its neck, and strolled up and down by the suspect's car, looking for all the world like any other citizen walking his pet in a residential neighborhood, while Hallinan waited nearby in an unmarked cruiser. When the suspect emerged from the building, the two detectives converged on him, reaching his car at the same moment he did.

Stein, on the passenger side, let the dog go and brought
his gun out across the hood, while Hallinan jumped out
of his car and put his gun into the man's neck. Hallinan
was still thinking the man might be Koehler, and when he
saw that he wasn't, he decided to frisk him anyway. In his
pocket, the man had a .22-caliber pistol with a silencer,
brass knuckles, rubber gloves, and a set of lock picks,
and in his car were two more silencer-equipped .22s.
Hallinan and Stein took him in and identified him as a
contract killer for drug operatives who was wanted for
several homicides. Later, tracing his phone calls, they
also succeeded in tracking down and capturing a fugitive
bank robber in Florida named Patty Huston, who was on
the FBI's ten-most-wanted list. "So Koehler got us a hit
man who was going out to kill somebody—probably
saved someone's life—and he got us Patty Huston," Hallinan said, adding, "There's an element of detective work
that they call luck."

Even in retirement, Hallinan kept a weather eye out
for Koehler, and for a time he had carried a copy of the
fugitive's Green Haven parole photo wherever he went. In
1992, when he was told the case was closed, he tore the
picture to shreds in frustration. But he had never been

convinced that Koehler was dead, so he was delighted that Rosenzweig wasn't, either.

"I don't know. It's not proven, Tom," Rosenzweig said. "We're gonna prove it, one way or the other." Hallinan told Rosenzweig everything he knew about the case, and then he cautioned him, as he had cautioned everyone else who'd called him about Koehler over the years. "Whoever's gonna take him, he's gonna be armed," Hallinan said. "Please pass that on. It's the one favor I ask of you."

ROSENZWEIG UNDERSTOOD Hallinan's warning. In his files, he had photocopies of Glennon and McGinn's toe tags from the city morgue, and he had read the medical examiner's reports of their autopsies. For Glennon, who was thirty-six, the cause of death was listed as "bullet wounds of arms, shoulder, thigh, chest, lungs, and heart"; and for McGinn, who was thirty-eight, it was listed as "bullet wounds of chest, arms, thigh, hand, heart, lungs, liver, intestines, right humerus and pelvis." Investigative work is by nature intrusive, and as if getting shot to death isn't enough of a violation to a body, an autopsy knows no shame. Every normality and abnormality of the dead men's bodies was described in detail: the track of each bullet through their flesh, bones, and organs; the quantity of mucus in their noses; the weight of their livers, spleens, lungs, hearts, and brains; the condition of their "external genitalia" (in both cases "unremarkable"); the strong smell of alcohol in their stomachs, which contained large amounts of "completely undigested food matter with recognizable fragments of meat and vegetables"; a fresh open bruise on McGinn's temple, which corresponded to witnesses' statements that he had been cut in his fight with Koehler at Channel Seven; and a large round bruise on the back of Glennon's neck marked by seven small grooves in "a patterned imprint of abrasions about one millimeter apart," which is a pathologist's way of saying that he had recently been bitten by another person.

Rosenzweig had also been studying the statement Koehler gave to police in 1945, when he was arrested for murder at the age of fifteen. The day before, Koehler and a sixteen-year-old friend named Billy Burns had visited Burns's girlfriend, Loretta Avalon, at her apartment in Chelsea. Burns showed Koehler a pearl, mounted on a half shell, that Avalon kept in a jar on her bureau and said was worth five hundred dollars. She also said she had a gun. Burns bet her two dollars that she didn't, and she reached under the bed, extracted a suitcase wrapped in a lady's slip, and brought out a .45-caliber Smith & Wesson six-shot revolver. The boys took turns handling the gun before Avalon stashed it away again. Then she asked them to take her dog for a walk, which they did, only, Koehler said, "Me and Billy didn't want to walk too far. We threw him in a car and left him there."

The next morning, Koehler and Burns returned to Avalon's apartment, kicked in the door, and took the pearl and the gun and a handful of costume jewelry. They stashed the loot in Burns's cellar, but a little while later when Koehler returned alone to their cache, he found it empty. "I felt sad," he said in his confession. "I didn't like it . . . I smelt something." He went looking for Burns, with the intention of "giving him a going-over," and when he caught up with him, he told him, "I got a buyer for the stuff." Burns said, "Let's wait a little while." That set Koehler off.

"I said, 'You punk, you know it ain't down there,' " he told the police. "Then I smacked him. Then he looked up at me sort of scared . . . I was pretty well sore. He said he gave it back to his girl. So I thought he was bull throwing me. I told him, 'Let's go over and knock off the YMCA.' So he said, 'All right.' So then he said to me, 'You're not mad at me, are you, Frankie?' I said, 'No, I ain't mad at you, Billy.' "

Koehler led Burns to a derelict loft building behind the YMCA on Twenty-third Street. They climbed up the fire escape and entered through a window on the second floor. Koehler let Burns walk ahead of him, then pulled out a gun—procured for him by Burns himself four months earlier at the Eighth Avenue fish market—and said, "If you don't tell me where the pearl is, I will blow your brains out." When Burns tried to run, Koehler shot him in the back from a distance of about five feet.

"He went down on one knee," Koehler told the cops. "He said, 'You shot me, Frankie.' I said, 'You bastard, you deserved it.' "

Before leaving Burns there to die, Koehler patted him down, hoping to find the pearl. But Burns didn't have it. He had told the truth when he said he returned it to his girlfriend. She had since handed the stolen goods over to the police as evidence, and it turned out the pearl was a fake, made of paste and glue, with a value of a dollar and sixty cents. Koehler was aware of these facts when he made his confessional statement, but he still seemed persuaded that he had been double-crossed. The closest he came to expressing remorse was to say, "I'm sorry now for a buck-sixty."

CHAPTER SIX

LATE IN THE EVENING of February 6, 1997, Rosenzweig
drove to Toms River, New Jersey, and, backed by a posse
of local policemen, knocked on Frank Fitzgerald's door.
The house was dark, and after a while he knocked again.
Eventually, lights came on, and a man in pajamas opened
the door. Rosenzweig recognized a sleep-struck version
of the face on Fitzgerald's driver's license.

"Frank?" he said.

"Yeah."

"Come here." Rosenzweig grabbed him by the collar. "You're under arrest for homicide."

"Homicide?! I never killed anyone. What are you talking about?"

"Are you Frank Koehler?"

"Nooo. Frank Fitzgerald."

"Are you sure?"

"Swear to God."

Rosenzweig was accustomed to remaining unmoved when people he arrested claimed that they hadn't done what he said they did or that they weren't who he thought they were. But Fitzgerald appeared genuinely bewildered. Rosenzweig let him go and followed him inside, accompanied by several colleagues. Fitzgerald didn't deny that he'd worked at the Coliseum and that there were plenty of bad guys there, but, he said, "You know what? I stayed away," and, "I mind my business." He was cooperative, producing documents to prove that he really was Frank Fitzgerald, and Rosenzweig noticed that he had no tattoos or scars where Koehler was said to have tattoos. Then Rosenzweig met Fitzgerald's wife, and he found himself thinking, They're the nicest couple.

Rosenzweig is not a religious man, but after twenty minutes, when he and his partners got up to leave, he said, "God bless you," and shook the Fitzgeralds' hands. "We were apologetic, as we should have been," he said. "It was a mistake, and sometimes you make mistakes—and it's not based on nothing."

In fact, Rosenzweig told me that the only time he had shot to kill he had done so as the result of a mistake. This was in 1969. He had noticed a man at "a known drug location" making a transaction in a men's room. When Rosenzweig accosted him, badge in hand, the guy made a run for it. Rosenzweig jumped on him, and they went down in "a fierce struggle." As they grappled on the men's room floor, Rosenzweig realized the man was stabbing at him with a bowie knife. His jacket had been slashed open. "I guess it's the closest I came—and I came close a few times—to getting badly injured or killed," he told me, and he said, "That was when I decided to shoot him." From a distance of no more than two feet, he fired directly into the man's chest and watched him fall away bleeding. But the wound was relatively minor. The man had been wearing a "miraculous medal" around his neck, and the medal had worked, catching the bullet and saving his life. Later, at the hospital, the man told Rosenzweig he hadn't been involved in a drug deal but was merely collecting a gambling debt. He hadn't cared to explain himself when Rosenzweig arrested him because what he saw was a cop coming at him and he figured the cop probably just wanted to rip him off—"which wasn't so far-fetched in those days," Rosenzweig said.

Still, Rosenzweig considered himself justified in shooting the man once they were on the floor and the knife was out, just as Tom Hallinan had felt justified in shooting the man who stabbed him in the face and Danny Lynch had been justified when the gangster Michael Sudia put a gun to his head and Lynch killed him. But with Hallinan and Lynch there had been no misunderstandings. Hallinan later found out that his attacker had already stabbed several security guards and a nurse at Bellevue Hospital, and by the time Hallinan drew his gun and wiped the blood from his eyes, the man had gone on to drive his knife through another cop's foot. "I could've finished him, but I did the nice thing. I put one in his knee, and I took the knife off him," Hallinan said. "He was out of the hospital before we were." And Lynch told me that when he had gone to see Sudia's body at the morgue, he had met Sudia's mother, who told him she had been making a novena, praying for her son to be stopped. "I wasn't too happy about being the one that stopped him, but I never felt a bit bad about it, neither," Lynch said. "I mean, this was a bad bastard, and he had this wonderful, sorrowful mother."

Rosenzweig's encounter with the man with the bowie knife and the miraculous medal offered no such consolations. What stuck with him afterward was not so much the fear that had inspired him to fire as what he called the "pit-in-my-stomach" recognition that "it was just a series of miscommunications, mistakes, misperceptions—on his part, and on my part—that had led to this." Most New York City policemen retire without ever having fired their guns at anyone, but a readiness to use force is at the core of what it means to be a cop. And thinking back on the shooting, Rosenzweig told me, "I don't think my career would have flourished if this happened now. There was a tolerance back then for people making mistakes—not mistakes of the heart, mistakes of the mind."

That tolerance is gone, Rosenzweig said. Yet, while the public calls for restraint, then complains, "What's happening? Crime's going up again. OK, let 'em loose again," he felt that the police department generally "does a very poor job of articulating what it's about: to go out on hot days, and in hot situations, and not only put your ass physically on the line—put your career on the line, put your reputation on the line, have your wife and your kids read in the news that you're under investigation, you're under arrest, you're under indictment, because you were out there, because people asked you, 'Get on that shield, go out there, and do that dirty job for us but don't do it a little too forcefully.' "

THE PEOPLE WHO have known Rosenzweig best over the years will tell you that if you really want to understand what he's all about, you should be aware that sometimes, when the drink is in him, he is given to singing the theme song from the movie *High Noon*:

Do not forsake me, oh my darlin' . . .

I do not know what fate awaits me
I only know I must be brave

And I must face a man who hates me
Or lie a coward, a craven coward
Or lie a coward in my grave.

In that movie, Gary Cooper plays Will Kane, a small-town western sheriff who learns on the morning he retires and gets married that an outlaw he sent to jail has been pardoned and is returning on the noon train to meet up with his gang and seek revenge. Kane pins his tin star back on and sets out to raise a posse against this prospect of mayhem. But the citizenry disappoints him—not a man is willing to risk his life—and Kane is left to make one of cinema's most stubborn, most starkly lonely stands in defense of a town for which, his face tells us, he has come to feel little more than disgust. That he prevails, with the last-minute help of his bride, who has been on the brink of abandoning him, only partially mitigates the film's presiding sense of desolation at the spinelessness that surrounds him. Barbarism has come within a pistol shot of swamping civilization, but there is no triumph for civilization. There is only Kane, an existential hero, yes, but with a peculiar twist; for, as he understands it, he does what he does not because he chooses to but because he feels he has no choice. "I've got to," he says. "That's the whole thing."

Rosenzweig himself will tell you that seeing *High Noon* as a teenager in the Bronx was one of the great inspirations of his life, but he will also tell you that after seeing the movie many times—and with Jack "One Punch" Minogue's "go the extra yard" speech fresh in his ears—he did not acquit himself as he might have liked when he first hit the streets as a cop. The summer of 1966, when Rosenzweig came on the job, was a season of riots and general unrest in the city, and he hardly had time to learn his way around the police academy before he was sent out on patrol. "Alone," he told me, and he repeated the word. "No partner, alone, no walkie-talkie, and—very important, your most important weapon, perhaps—no knowledge of the law. You've been in the academy a couple days and you're out in the street. You're some kind of I don't know what—a Hessian, or a soldier, an occupying force, just someone in a uniform, and a gun, looking for trouble. So now you have young Officer Rosenzweig, twenty-one years old, on Forty-third Street

and Eighth Avenue, by the New York Times, and someone tells me, 'Officer, there's a guy causing trouble up the
street.'

"So I go up the street, and here's a guy a good half a
head taller than me and maybe forty pounds heavier, and
he's harassing people. He's just being a pain in the ass.
He's not assaulting anyone but he's acting disorderly.
He was a discon"—disorderly conduct—"arrest if I knew
what I was doing. But I was scared. I was definitely
scared. I walk up to him, and I tell him, 'Hey, cut it out,
and move along.' And he uses some expletive. And—'I'm
telling you to move along'—I'm trying to exert my authority as an officer. I have, like, half the right instincts, but I
had only half of them. So I then say to him, 'Listen, I'm
gonna walk back around the corner. If you're here when I
get back, I'm gonna lock you up.' And he may have used
some other expletive, and I walked away.

"And I didn't come back," Rosenzweig declared.
"And it was a rather craven thing to do." The next evening, off duty, he stopped in, as was his habit, at Chambers'
bar and sat down to drink beside Dave Cody, a narcotics
detective nearly twice his age whom he looked up to as a

mentor. "We were having drinks. Having drinks. Having drinks," Rosenzweig recalled, his voice slowing a bit to imply the rhythm of the rounds. As the evening progressed, Rosenzweig had confessed, "Dave, I had a situation last night," and he told his story. Cody was not sympathetic. "You can't ever fucking do that," he said. "Don't ever do that if you want to be a cop. There's other careers. People are depending on you. You let people down there."

"I felt that small," Rosenzweig told me, holding a hand a few inches from the floor. "No, I felt much smaller than that. I felt totally diminished."

A few years later, during a crackdown on police corruption by the United States Attorney's office, Dave Cody was subpoenaed to testify against some of his colleagues in the Special Investigations Unit. Instead he drove to a park in Riverdale and shot himself. "One of a number of guys I knew who couldn't deal with life," Rosenzweig said. "That's part of the deal when you go into this work—you see people severely affected, and sometimes they lose their lives in different ways. It scars you." He didn't dwell on the matter, except to say, "I wasn't easy to live with. My first wife deserves credit." He preferred to remember how his own failings as a novice cop had drawn Cody's scolding. "Oh God, was that an important lesson for me," he said. "I didn't back down after that."

Of course, there was such a thing as being too gung ho, and as a young sergeant in the early 1970s, Rosenzweig had taken what were then unprecedented measures to have a compulsively aggressive officer expelled from the force as psychologically unfit for police work. "From the start, this guy booked a lot of resisting-arrest charges, which is a pretty good sign that he's using his hands too much," he said. He recalled his vigilance in that matter with pride, and yet, twenty years later, he was relieved when his own son decided not to become a cop. The climate had changed, he told me, but the deeper problem remained: "You're given this position of authority, you're supposed to enforce the laws, you're supposed to protect the public, and now you're in this situation where you have to arrest someone because you have probable cause to believe they committed a crime. They don't want to be arrested, and now they resist you. How much force can you use? Is a punch in the mouth OK? Can you hit him on the head with the nightstick? Can you just jab him in the belly? Everything you do is going to look brutal to someone watching. You have to use a minimum amount of force. But what is a minimum? Do you have to use so little force that he gets the best of you, and gets your gun away from you and kills you?"

Think about it, Rosenzweig said. "I'm not talking about Abner Louima, or the Rodney King case—gratuitous violence against people. I'm talking about people that have to do their jobs. It's not a pleasant thing."

Since matter cannot move without disturbing other matter along its path, there always is—there must be—a trail of some sort.

—DASHIELL HAMMETT
"HOUSE DICK"

CHAPTER SEVEN

AS THE WINTER of 1997 gave way to spring, and then summer, Andy Rosenzweig used to tell his friends that on account of his obsession with Frankie Koehler, he was afraid Mary was about to become his third ex-wife. He was only partially joking. Following his dead-end excursion to New Jersey, he started taking Mary to eat at the Skylight Diner on the corner of Thirty-fourth Street and Ninth Avenue because Koehler's brother, Kenny, lived up the block. Rosenzweig figured that if Frankie Koehler happened to be alive and in a visiting mood, he might come into Penn Station by train and walk right past the diner's plate-glass window. "You never know," he said.

At the same time, Rosenzweig asked two men from his squad—Tommy Pon, a thirty-eight-year-old senior investigator whom Rosenzweig called "a surveillance wiz," and Chris Donohue, a twenty-eight-year-old "apple-cheeked, spanky-clean-looking rookie"—to watch Kenny Koehler and to make sure they weren't seen doing so. "Just eyeball, no chatting," he said. "We'd taken a risk with that Jersey thing, and it could've gotten out at that point that we're still looking at this case." He didn't even tell Pon and Donohue why he was interested in Kenny, lest they "go on a tangent." But when they returned with excellent photographs and a succinct report of the man's unremarkable daily activities, Rosenzweig gave them the file on Frankie. "I'm assigning you this case," he said, "and keep in mind, the whole time you do this, you may find out nothing more than this guy is dead."

Rosenzweig also decided it was time to enlist the official support and subpoena power of a prosecutor, and he turned to Steve Saracco, a veteran assistant district attorney who, with his partner Dan Bibb, worked exclusively

Andy Rosenzweig at the Skylight Diner.
Photograph by Gilles Peress

on cold homicide cases. Saracco took an immediate liking to the Koehler story, with its legacy of frustration and
neglect. In cold-case work, he told me, "The majority of
cases we look at are not what I believe Thomas Pynchon
called glamor grudges. They have *no* profile." And, he
said, "There's a lot of failure."

The investigation now consisted largely in retracing
the steps of previous investigations: constructing an up-
to-date Koehler family tree, subpoenaing Koehler family
phone records, tracing the calls, and determining each
time a phone number was attached to a name with a criminal record if that name might be an alias for Frankie.
"Painstaking," Rosenzweig said. At one point, Pon and
Donohue observed Kenny Koehler buying marijuana in a
city park, which allowed them to pick him up without
leading him to suspect they were really interested in his
brother. At the precinct house, they went through his address book, which gave them even more numbers to work
with, including one for a man identified only as Tex, who
lived in the Brighton Beach area of Brooklyn. That was
promising: one of the few bits of information on the rap
sheet from Frankie Koehler's first arrest, in 1944, was the
entry Alias Tex. "I had Mary check that number, forward,

backward, inside out, upside down, coded, decoded," Rosenzweig told me, "and each one of those was then a lead that had to be followed—all for naught."

By early summer, there was little left to investigate in the New York area, and Rosenzweig and his men turned their attention to a branch of Koehler's family in California. Rosenzweig was particularly intrigued by a pair of Koehler's nephews there, brothers called McMullen, each of whom had been arrested dozens of times: "Burglary, arson, assault—no murders, but these were legitimate full-time criminals." Not surprisingly, one of the McMullens was in a California jail at the time, and Rosenzweig had Pon get in touch with a local prison investigator to monitor his outside phone calls. "These guys know they're being taped," Rosenzweig said. "They have a sign up—THESE CALLS ARE TAPED—but they still talk."

The imprisoned McMullen never said anything "particularly inculpatory," but from what Rosenzweig could make out in the prison investigator's reports, there were hints of an uncle somewhere in his orbit. "It wasn't so clear," Rosenzweig told me, "but these guys are criminals; it's a logical conclusion. Who's their role model gonna be? It's not gonna be Philip Gourevitch or Andy

Rosenzweig. It's not gonna be John Gotti; he's from a different era and milieu. It's gonna be Frankie Koehler, their criminal uncle."

Koehler's sixty-eighth birthday was coming up on July 24, and Rosenzweig decided it was "worth a shot" to send Pon and Donohue out to California for the occasion to watch the McMullen brother who wasn't in jail and see where he might lead them. His name was Danny; he lived in Benicia, a tranquil, low-crime hamlet of twenty-eight thousand people that sits just below the southern tip of Napa Valley, about a forty-five-minute drive from San Francisco; and what he did on Koehler's birthday was beat up his common-law wife, threaten to stab her and her son, and get arrested one more time.

Pon and Donohue had hooked up with a local FBI agent named Pete French, and together they took advantage of McMullen's trouble to question his battered wife, his building manager, and some of his neighbors. "We decided to risk heating up the place, as we call it—reach out to some folks and see if they could help us," French recalled. "Good, bad, or indifferent, when you identify yourself as an FBI agent it tends to get people's attention." French's presence also allowed Pon and Donohue not to mention that they were from New York as they showed Koehler's old pictures around. But nobody they spoke with claimed to recognize him, and McMullen's wife insisted that it was news to her that her husband had such an uncle. The investigators poked about for several hours, then they called Rosenzweig's office to report negative results and to ask: Should they now check out Frank O'Grady?

"Who's he?" Rosenzweig said. His men explained that Danny McMullen listed two references on his apartment-rental agreement: a relative in southern California and a Frank O'Grady, who lived at the Benicia Inn, a low-rent residential hotel for "people in transient situations." Rosenzweig said, "Go," and the next day, which was a Friday, Pon, Donohue, and French knocked on O'Grady's door. A man opened it, and when he gave his name, Pon and Donohue recognized him as one of Koehler's nephews from New York. French then introduced himself as a federal agent.

"Where's Frank O'Grady?" he said, and Koehler's nephew told him, "He's down in Reno, gambling. It's his birthday."

CHAPTER EIGHT

WHEN ROSENZWEIG CAME into his office on Monday morning, he found Tommy Pon and Chris Donohue in a despondent mood. They were 99 percent sure that O'Grady was Koehler; they'd been so close—Donohue had felt the hair stand up on the back of his scalp at the Benicia Inn—and they'd blown their cover. Rosenzweig refused to join in their spirit of failure. After all, nobody had "got a sniff" of Koehler in twenty-seven years, and, he said, "You pretty much proved he's alive. That's what we wanted to do. We're going to get this guy." Of course, Rosenzweig, too, was thinking, Where? When? But he felt for the first time, after six months on the case, that he had something more than faith to go on. "If we're gonna have a lot more work to do," he told his men, "we'll do a lot more work."

In the meantime, Pete French had returned to Benicia with some colleagues from the FBI, and they did not bother to be inconspicuous. Rather, with their guns on display, they worked their way up and down First Street, Benicia's main thoroughfare, and learned that the man who called himself Frank O'Grady—or, formally, Edward Francis O'Grady—was a beloved and ubiquitous character in the town. People called him New York Frankie, on account of his thick Hell's Kitchen accent, and the Mayor of Downtown, because he spent his days walking from the Benicia Inn at one end of First Street to the old Tannery Building, where he worked as a part-time custodian, at the other end, and then back again, lingering for hours along the way, drinking coffee and chatting with the regulars at the Union Hotel and, especially, at the town's main café, In the Company of Wolves. He was spoken of as a generous, community-spirited man, always ready to help people in need and kind to children and small animals. He was an occasional small-time trader in the town's busy antiques market, and for a while there had been talk of his opening a New York–style delicatessen with Deb and Deb, the lesbian proprietors of In the Company of Wolves. But he'd never been one for full-time work; he had no Social Security number and no driver's license, and he spent many solitary hours fishing off the town pier or combing the ragged beaches of the East Bay for old sea glass.

Frank O'Grady had arrived in Benicia in the mid-1970s with a wife, who was also a New Yorker, and for most of the time since then he had lived with her in a small house she had purchased downtown. But for the past three years, he had been living at the Benicia Inn with a girlfriend named Dolores Kenyon, although he had continued to see his wife almost daily. French and his FBI colleagues called on both women, and with warrants in hand, they searched their homes and carted away many of their personal papers. O'Grady's wife told them she had no idea where he was. Kenyon, who had gone to Reno with him for his birthday, told them O'Grady had received a phone call there on Friday night that had upset him and he'd then left her at their hotel, saying he had to take care of some business.

When French called New York on Tuesday afternoon, he told Pon that Frank O'Grady was definitely Frankie Koehler. Nobody in Benicia had exactly volunteered this information; in fact, French said, very few people knew. Rather, he told me, "After we'd talked to a lot of people, one piece of information combined with another and another, and these bits of information were things that even people who knew Koehler hadn't put together. He was somewhat successful at not giving information to people. He held his mud. And his family held their mud as well. Why? I can't say whether it's because they feared him or loved him."

That evening, according to habit, Rosenzweig took Mary to the Skylight Diner on West Thirty-fourth Street. "You never know," he told her, and she said, "Oh, yeah, here we go again." They sat by the window, and as Mary predicted, they saw nothing suspicious. But the next day, Wednesday, July 30, around three in the afternoon, Rosenzweig's patronage of the Skylight was at least partially vindicated when his office phone rang and his deputy, Joe Pennisi, told him that an agent from the New York office of the FBI had just reported that Frankie Koehler was believed to be arriving at Penn Station on Amtrak train No. 48, due in at 3:41 p.m.

Rosenzweig didn't know it then, but Pete French had gone back to Benicia that morning to question more people and had learned that Koehler had not, in fact, left Reno on Friday night. He'd stayed there with Dolores Kenyon, and on Saturday she'd driven him to Martinez, a town next to Benicia. Then, on Sunday morning, she had said goodbye to him at the Martinez train station after he bought a ticket to New York. French had contacted Amtrak and learned that the California Zephyr out of San Francisco made such a connection, through Chicago, with the Lake Shore Limited into Penn Station —a seventy-three-and-a-half-hour trip—and, yes, an E. F. O'Grady was on the passenger list.

The time difference between the coasts was such that French in California had put all the pieces together only in the hour before the train's scheduled arrival in New York, and he had been holding two phones to his head, speaking simultaneously with Amtrak and with the FBI's

Manhattan office. French also faxed some copies of recent photographs of Koehler to the D.A.'s office, but Rosenzweig and his men were already gone.

ROSENZWEIG, PENNISI, AND PON reached Penn Station almost exactly at the moment when the train was supposed to pull in. An Amtrak police captain was waiting for them with the good news that the train was running ten minutes late. Rosenzweig asked him to have the train stopped short of the station. "We don't do that," the man said. "Too worried about hostage situations." Rosenzweig decided there was no time to argue policy. The train was already out of the Hudson River tunnel, jogging over the last few hundred yards of track into the station.

Four escalators connected the arrival platform to the main terminal, and with his posse fortified by the police captain and four other Amtrak employees, that meant Rosenzweig could station two men on each. None of them knew what Koehler might look like.

When Rosenzweig told me about the moment he watched the train doors open from his post on the platform, he didn't say much. He sat forward on his chair, craning his neck in a searching way, and his eyes ticked

frantically from side to side as he saw again the oncom-
ing rush of travelers and tried to pick out a murderer
whom he felt he knew intimately but whom he had never
seen, except in a thirty-five-year-old photograph and a
computer-assisted portrait he had no reason to trust. "Till
my dying day, I won't know for sure, but I think he
walked right by me," he told me, adding, "There were so
many people. I'll always be regretful that I didn't grab
him."

After the last passengers had cleared off the platform,
Rosenzweig searched the train. There were a few strag-
glers, and he found someone sleeping in a bathroom but
nobody who looked like Koehler. Rosenzweig finally gave
up. He got on an escalator, wishing he'd moved on the
man who'd caught his eye and thinking, It was a sign, I'm
ready to retire, I'm losing my edge. Then he heard an
Amtrak policeman say, "They got him, up in the cell
in the office," and, he told me, "I went up there, just ju-
bilant."

At the foot of one escalator, Tommy Pon had spotted a
sturdy old man with scruffy gray hair wearing a gray
baseball cap and gray sweatshirt, carrying a suitcase in
one hand and in his other hand holding a handkerchief

Frank Koehler in his 1962 parole photograph (above), *in the FBI's computer-"aged" portrait* (right, above), *and on the day of his arrest, July 30, 1997* (right, below)

over his mouth and chin, as if he were about to cough into it. Pon got behind him to study him more closely. He saw that the man's left ear was cauliflowered, as Koehler's appeared to be in his old parole photograph, and he also noticed that while everyone else on the escalator faced forward, his man kept looking this way and that. At the top of the escalator, their eyes met and locked momentarily in mutual recognition. Pon was struck by the look of disgust that confronted him, and he signaled to an Amtrak detective standing nearby.

"You got me," Koehler said when they seized him. "It's over." Rosenzweig later said, "It should have been me catching this guy, if it was a true-crime novel," but he repeatedly praised Pon, Donohue, and French. "I may have been the architect," he said, "but they were the craftsmen who completed the job."

The holding cell at the Amtrak police office was just big enough for two people to sit facing each other. Rosenzweig was so eager to get in there that he had to be reminded to follow the standard procedure for any officer entering any cell in America and take off his gun. Then, he told me, "I walked in, and said, 'You're Frank Koehler.' No one had used the name yet. He said, 'It's been a long time since anyone called me that. It feels kind of good, though.'

"I said, 'My name's Andy Rosenzweig, and I've been thinking about you for quite a long time.'

"He said, 'Oh, yeah?'

"I said, 'Yeah, you're under arrest for the murder of Richie Glennon and Pete McGinn.'

"I said, 'I want to advise you of your rights.'

"He said, 'I know my rights, don't bother.'

"I said, 'I want to advise you. Everybody has to be advised of his rights.'

"He said, 'What can I tell ya? If you got witnesses, I'm fucked.'

"I said, 'We got witnesses.'

"He said, 'Well, then I'm fucked.' "

PART TWO

Reckoning

Is a rattle-snake accountable?

—HERMAN MELVILLE
THE CONFIDENCE MAN

CHAPTER NINE

ONCE AGAIN, FRANKIE KOEHLER was a prisoner. But as he understood it, he had not been caught; rather, he'd surrendered. In his suitcase, he had been carrying a .380 semiautomatic handgun loaded with hollow-point bullets, and as Rosenzweig drove him downtown to the D.A.'s office, he declared that he had intended to use it. "I saw you guys, every one of you, on the platform. I thought of taking a few of you, and then doing this." He made a pistol of his forefinger and thumb and put it to his forehead.

"But I figured, Aw, what's the point now? I'm old. You guys probably have families. So maybe I got a little religion. I met some nice people on the train."

Rosenzweig was glad to find Koehler talkative. "Interrogation is a process," he said, and he considered the murderer's "philosophical" tone a promising overture. "Even though this was a guy who had killed someone I knew quite well, I wasn't surprised that I didn't feel a great deal of emotion," he told me. "I didn't feel hatred. I don't function on that level. Policemen can't afford to." He decided to leave the prisoner alone while he was fingerprinted at the D.A.'s office, to allow him time to contemplate his predicament before further questioning.

Then Rosenzweig began by letting Koehler understand how much he knew about his family life, his parents, his siblings, his nieces and nephews, and many details about his background, including some about his affairs with women. Koehler made clear he would prefer to keep his adulterous escapades secret. Rosenzweig didn't press these sensitive matters. He just wanted Koehler to consider the number of people close to him who could be affected by his capture. He said, "Let me ask you something. You're sixty-eight years old. Where were you going to go?"

Koehler told him that he still knew some people in New York and had planned, with their help, to get a few thousand dollars, a new identity, and a new hairstyle. Then he was going to call the *Newsday* columnist Jimmy Breslin and tell him to write that he, Frankie Koehler, was going to kill a cop a day unless, or until, the FBI promised to stay away from his family. "And I would've done it," he said. "It'd be easy."

"We got you now, Frank," Rosenzweig said. "So why don't you give it up? Why don't you try to help yourself a little bit." Koehler said he didn't want any help; all he wanted was for the feds to lay off his wife and family. When Rosenzweig promised to tell the feds to do that, Koehler slapped the table. "What do you want to know?" he asked, and Rosenzweig suggested, "Tell me about the homicides."

Koehler didn't hold back; he described the killing of Glennon and McGinn with a vividness that seemed to erase the intervening years. And that same evening, he said it all again to the prosecutor, Steve Saracco, in a videotaped confession that has come to be regarded at the D.A.'s office as one of the classic portraits of a criminal personality.

ON THE TAPE, Koehler sits alone at a large table, wearing the cap and sweatshirt he had on when he was captured. At first, he appears hunched and restless. His head tilts down, and his blue eyes, underslung by heavy bags, stare out. His hands drum at the table. In every way, his posture and gestures imply sullen forbearance, even boredom, as he is advised once again of his legal rights. But when, at his request, Saracco repeats Rosenzweig's promise, "There is going to be nothing done against your wife," Koehler sits up straight. His face opens. He raps the table, takes off his glasses, and holds his hands outspread before him, as if to say, Come on in.

Koehler does not require much prompting to relate the twenty-seven-year-old story of what he calls his "beef" with his victims. He says, "I'm gonna tell you everything what I can remember with the booze," and he appears to have forgotten nothing. He admits it was wrong to have fooled around with the wife of a man who was "in the can." But, he claims, he had settled the matter—"when the man came home, I told him, told him he could do whatever he wanted about it, put my hands down, told him he could punch me in the face if he wanted to"—and Glennon and McGinn had no business reproaching him for the affair.

He does not glamorize his own performance in his fight with McGinn: "When I turned he caught me in the nose. I wasn't in too good shape after that. He threw a punch that I grabbed his hand. I tried to bite his fucking finger off." In the end, he says, "I was down on the ground, I must've went out from a kick in the head." While he lay there, he claims, Glennon stripped his wedding ring from his finger, and when he got up and went back into the bar, he and Glennon exchanged words: "He told me he had a gun on him, or something, he would shoot me, some stupid shit." Then, Koehler says, "I went somewhere. I ain't gonna tell you where 'cause I'm not involving any other people. I picked up a pistol. It was a P-.38."

His voice, smoke-gruffened, with its whining *r*s ("woid" for "word," "noive" for "nerve," "hoit" for "hurt"), its kicking *d*s for *th*s ("dis," "dat," and "dose"), and its adamant, shoving rhythms, is pure old New

York—so pure that it now sounds foreign in the very city it came from. For Koehler is a refugee of sorts from the white, hoodlum milieu of another time and from a city that no longer really exists. "A period piece," Rosenzweig called him, "the ultimate West Side bad guy." But it is less his accent than the attitude of his speech that defines Koehler's sensational performance in the D.A.'s video. He calls himself "a professional criminal," yet, far from being on the defensive, he appears almost to relish bearing witness against himself—not confessing so much as taking credit for his crimes.

"So you left the bar to get a gun?" Saracco asks.

That's right, Koehler says, "Premeditated murder, yeah. Don't worry about it, I'll give you every fucking thing you want."

"I'm not gonna put any words in your mouth," Saracco tells him.

"I know. I'm talking. I went and got some pistol, loaded it up, went back to the bar, and said, 'Hey, jeez, you know, I wanna talk, let's talk this over. We're all friends.' "

Once again, Koehler says, Glennon taunted him: " 'You hurt anybody, I'll testify against you,' " and, " 'I got a gun on me.' " Koehler felt baited but unimpressed. He makes the noises "Rrrrrrr" and "Aaaaaaa" to imitate Glennon, as if he'd heard his words as nothing more than the buzzing of an overwrought insect inviting a swatting. When Saracco asks him if his victims posed any threat to him with guns, Koehler says, "No." After all, he explains, "They were scared about me. McGinn especially was worried." Saracco asks why they were worried, and he says, "Maybe they thought I was dangerous."

"Did they have a reason to think you were dangerous?" Saracco asks.

"Yeah."

"And what would that reason be?"

"I am dangerous," Koehler says. "I'm dangerous."

Yet he insists the killings were not inevitable. When he and Glennon arrived at McGinn's apartment, he says, "I still hadn't made up my mind to hurt anybody." In fact, as he tells it, everything might have been fine if "Glennon with his fucking mouth" had kept quiet. "Even though I had a fight with McGinn, you gotta understand I was more mad at Glennon," he says, and he repeatedly comes back to this point, explaining that he had despised the man for years and groping to articulate why.

"McGinn, I didn't give a fuck whether he lived or died," but, "Glennon I wanted fucking dead." Koehler's hand jabs the air to emphasize each word, but twenty-seven years after he killed both men, his antipathy toward Glennon seems overwhelming. All he can say is, "He was a scumbag. He was a piece of shit . . . I didn't *like* this guy. He was an annoyance. I'm trying to explain it as best I can."

Koehler has no trouble, however, describing the scene in McGinn's apartment. He and McGinn were seated on a couch attempting to talk to each other, he says, but Glennon—"Mr. Tough Guy"—kept interrupting, talking about his gun, saying, "You could be shot," and when he was told to shut up, "He said something about his day in the sun." Koehler wasn't exactly sure what Glennon meant, and he didn't bother to ask. "That done something in my head," he tells Saracco. "I cocked the gun, got up, hit him in the gut." Koehler pats his right abdomen, just over the appendix, to indicate the spot where the first bullet entered Glennon. "Caved him in good. But he stood up. That son of a bitch stood . . . I said to him, 'Does that hurt?' He didn't answer me. I hit him twice more in the chest. He went down." Koehler's phrases slip suddenly into the present tense: "I'm pounding on him now. He's a dead man. I ain't worried about him. I ain't worried about nothing. I'm pissed. And he's gonna die. And he died."

As for McGinn, Koehler tells Saracco, "If he would have sat still, he would've been OK."

"You would have walked out the door and let him live?"

"Yeah. What the fuck? I'm not after him. This is not a personal thing."

But McGinn had risen from his seat, saying, " 'What did you do? What did you do?' " That made Koehler "a little angry again," and he got angrier still when McGinn began to raise his hands. "I said, 'You ain't gonna make it,' and I whacked him. I whacked him. I shot him in the belly. He went down. Now I'm pissed off. I gotta tell you, I was very angry. 'So,' I said, 'so you thought this was a fucking joke, you scumbag.' And I hit him twice in the back."

"When he's down?" Saracco asks.

"Yeah."

"Did he say anything to you? Did he plead for his life?"

"I think he moaned. I think I knew he was dying. I think I heard this moan—when you're just about to check out, you know."

Koehler says he was barely conscious at first that he had also shot McGinn's uncle Charlie: "When I clipped him, he went down . . . I didn't even know who he was. I had no beef at all with him." But a little later, he says, "I think I sort of remember the old man you're talking about. He walked into the hallway or something, and I think I might have popped him. I hit him in the leg, right, and he crawled out on me?"

"I wasn't there," Saracco reminds him.

"Well, smart move," Koehler replies. "He crawled out on me, 'cause I looked for him. In fact, that sort of saved everything, 'cause that panicked me." Until then, he says, he'd been imagining that "if there was nobody else left, I'd have gone back to the bar," as though murdering the proprietor and his best friend had been a casual errand, like stepping out for a pack of smokes. But remembering Uncle Charlie, he thought, "Oh, that fuck got out on me, I'm in trouble, I'm in deep shit," and it occurred to him that he'd better get out, too.

So, when he finished shooting McGinn, Koehler went

quickly through Glennon's pockets and found that he had been carrying a gun but no bullets—"no clip in it, unloaded." Koehler took it anyway, then fired two more shots into Glennon's corpse, and he was headed for the door when Glennon's girlfriend came in from the hallway. This presented him with a dilemma.

"What am I gonna do?" he asks. "Whack her? No, I'm not gonna do that. I'm not gonna whack somebody I'm not fucking mad at. What the fuck would I do that for?" Koehler later suggests that shooting her may not have been an option, because he had used all his bullets. But what really seems to matter to him is his power to decide who lives and who dies. McGinn and Glennon are dead, he says, because "I wanted to kill them." And he says, "Where I come from, when you don't like someone, really don't like 'em, and they're fucking scumbags, you shoot them. It's no mystery, you know. I don't shoot people for nothing."

BUT IT IS a mystery. Try as he might—and he does not shrink from the challenge—Koehler cannot really account for himself. Indeed, for all his self-dramatization, he does not question his own murderousness. On the contrary, he appears fascinated by the idea of himself as a dealer of fate. When Saracco asks him about his brother, Kenny, Koehler calls him "a punk," and remarks, inexplicably, "He's alive because I'm very generous. You can tell that cocksucker that when you see him . . . If I didn't love his kids, I'd whack him in the fucking head. He would've been dead long ago." Later, speaking of his unrealized "plan" to shoot his way through Penn Station, then kill a cop a day with the columnist Jimmy Breslin as his medium, Koehler again expresses the desire to be understood not only as a murderer but also as a sparer of life. Saracco comments, "It's very fortunate nothing went down at the train today," and Koehler leans toward his interrogator and tells him, "My choice, OK."

He seems to regard the fact that he resisted the urge to take his gun out of his suitcase before leaving the train as evidence that he has reformed. As a fugitive, he says, he had lived by the principle "Somebody gets in my way I gotta take 'em down," and in order to avoid such trouble, "I stayed out of criminal activity completely." He hadn't been afraid of getting shot himself at Penn Station—"If I gotta die, I gotta die, that's life"—but the prospect of "popping people all over the joint" to preserve his freedom had finally lost its appeal. A new idea had taken its place in his mind. Leaving the train, Koehler had found himself thinking, People gotta live.

Even now as a prisoner, recalling the ecstatic rage with which he has killed in the past, he remains tenderized by the conviction that he has granted extended life to countless others by checking what he calls "the instinct in me." He says, "It's a bad situation—on the run—it's fucked-up. You can't rob a joint, or get a beef, or a pinch. So you're gonna hurt people. I don't want to hurt anybody else. I'm tired of it, and I'm not mad at anybody . . . I don't want no fucking medals for it—no medals 'cause I'm a nice fellow. It's just that on the train it was a good ride. I met a lot of nice people."

By the end of the video, he seems genuinely unburdened, even pleased with himself. "Thank you, Mr. Koehler," Steve Saracco says, and at the sound of his name, Koehler smiles. "I forgot who the fuck I was for twenty-seven years," he says. "OK, nice meeting you . . . have a nice life."

CHAPTER TEN

"AND THEY SAY people mellow with age," Andy Rosenzweig said after we watched the Koehler video together.
He didn't doubt that Koehler had led a peaceable existence in Benicia, but he also didn't care. The man had
presented himself just as Rosenzweig had expected:
armed, bloody-minded, and without a jot of remorse.
"The fact that he didn't snap at Penn Station doesn't
make him a less dangerous person," he said. "Most of us,
walking around, haven't killed anyone. He has—repeat-

edly and efficiently—and he came into town prepared to
do it again."

Still, Rosenzweig told me, "In my time with Koehler,
in my office, I did see a flicker of humanity. It was when I
told him that he'd left Pete McGinn's four children fatherless. You had to be looking very closely, but I could
see just a little facial twitch. There was something still in
this guy. He wasn't completely a monster, just a murderer. And I took some encouragement from that. If there
was any level, however minuscule, on which he felt he'd
done wrong, there was at least a chance that he might co-
operate and not fight this case in court."

Yes, Koehler had confessed, but his case remained
open, and Rosenzweig was eager to avoid the legal ma-
neuvering and uncertainty of a trial, where there was a
possibility that the videotape could be thrown out on
technical grounds. There was no way of calculating that
risk precisely, but Steve Saracco and his cold-case partner Dan Bibb agreed that it would be best not to run it.
Koehler's double homicide was by far the oldest crime for
which they had ever brought an indictment, and as Bibb
said, "Generally, age is not good for a case." Of course,
there were still witnesses. But McGinn's uncle Charlie

had recently died, so the prosecutors would have to depend heavily on the testimony of Glennon's girlfriend, who remained traumatized by her memories and might get wobbly under pressure. Moreover, Koehler's lawyer, Murray Richman, a criminal defender whose client list includes many of the city's leading mobsters, had a reputation as a fiercely unforgiving needler during cross-examination. Although Saracco and Bibb believed they could win a conviction even without Koehler's confession, they preferred not to give Richman a chance to persuade a jury to let the murderer walk.

MURRAY RICHMAN'S APPEARANCE on the scene puzzled Rosenzweig. Koehler, who had no money to speak of, had at first been assigned a Legal Aid lawyer, and Richman, who is among the city's most expensive criminal lawyers, does not believe in pro bono work. "Reasonable doubt begins with the payment of a reasonable fee," he likes to say, and, "The rich need representation, too," and his successful defense of successful criminals has made him, true to his name, a rich man. Rosenzweig had first crossed paths with him thirty years earlier, in the Four-One Precinct, where Richman had been born and raised and was starting out as a lawyer when Rosenzweig came on the job as a cop. They were both Jews, both sons of the Bronx and of working-class, immigrant fathers (Richman's was a Bessarabian-born housepainter), both street-smart and just plain smart, both making their names in the law—and, beyond that, they could not have been more different. Richman was a swashbuckler, backslapping, fast-talking, scrappy, and brash. He reveled in his association with outlaws. Don't Worry Murray they called him as he made the rounds of their nightclubs, their restaurants, their weddings, their wakes, dealing out business cards, saying, Talk to me, Listen to me, Don't worry, I'll take care of it. In fact, Rosenzweig himself had once hired Richman as his lawyer.

"An instructive experience," he said. "This was in 1970, when me and my first wife bought our first house. I'd run into Murray in court, and mentioned we were looking in Rockland County, where he lived. He said, 'I'll handle the closing,' and—what a character—I remember he said, 'I'm a real-estate genius.' OK, fine. He sent us to an agent, who showed us a little raised ranch we liked in West Nyack. Just before we moved in, we went to a house party down the block. I was sitting next to this guy, and he started laughing. He said, 'Pretty funny, a cop moving in across from the Mafia.' No kidding, there was a mob family facing our house. Husband and wife were both under indictment, and guess who was representing them? You know who. I asked my captain, 'Should I *not* buy this place?' He said, 'Aw, it's OK.' But I always thought it was weird. What the hell was Murray trying to do?"

Since then, Rosenzweig had been inclined to believe that where Richman was concerned, it was best to presume nothing was as innocent as it seemed. Not that he suspected the lawyer of anything untoward when it came to Koehler; but he couldn't imagine how Koehler had found his way into Richman's hands except through the sort of local organized-crime contacts he claimed to have severed when he fled New York.

Sure enough, when I called on Richman at his office in the Bronx, he told me that Koehler had been put in touch with him by a dear old friend and client—"a mob guy . . . a very very tough guy . . . a guy I really love"— who had been convicted of murder when he was sixteen and spent twenty-two years in jail, where he and Koehler had met and forged an enduring bond. Richman had kept his friend out of jail ever since, and in exchange, his friend had helped Richman build his business, referring a steady stream of clients. "He was a guy who mixed in," he said. "He had a lot of friends, and all you really need are a couple big ones like that and suddenly you're a hero, and you have a following." Richman didn't doubt that although Koehler had kept out of trouble, he had also kept a hand in "the life" during his sojourn in California. "He had something going. There's no question," he told me, adding, "Did he not commit crimes? I can't say that. Did he not get caught? That's staying out of trouble, you know. I do believe he was into other things. And by the very fact that he was able to reach my friend, I knew he had to be into other things, because my friend is into a lot of things."

Richman agreed to represent Koehler after some of Koehler's nephews in New York agreed to pay him a fee of about twenty-five thousand dollars, and even when the nephews stopped paying—"gave me a couple of checks, and their consciences were salved, that was the end of it, shitty people"—he stayed with the case. By then he had taken a liking to Koehler, and he said, "What am I going to do, start suing? Frank was all by himself. I really felt compassion for him." He called Koehler "a fascination" and "a lovable rogue," and he said, "You can't call him a sweet guy, but he's a lot less dumber than I took him for at first . . . He's one of the smartest guys I've ever seen."

Richman allowed that killing Glennon and McGinn was "the dumbest thing—dumb—just sheer stupidity," but he took some comfort in the fact that Koehler was drunk at the time: "That's not an excuse for the murders, but it may reduce the murder charge. If you have inability to form intent, if things happen because you're out of control, it may not be murder. It could be manslaughter. Could be a lot of other things. Could be diminished capacity." Under the circumstances, Richman said, Koehler did have a defense—"lack of *mens rea* because of alcohol"—or so he thought until he watched the D.A.'s videotape.

Koehler had told his lawyer that he had made his confession under duress after Rosenzweig had threatened to drag his wife into the case. Richman's attitude was: too bad. "What was improper about that statement?" he said. "Was there a gun placed to his head? Was he forced to make that statement? He virtually volunteered the statement. Nobody threatened him. You tell me how I was going to get that suppressed. I didn't see any basis. Under

The People v. *Huntley*, which is the basis for suppression, you need some coercion. Even trick and device is OK. You can trick somebody into a statement, and it's valid. They're entitled to do that. That's perfectly proper. There's no reason why not—'You don't fess up, I'll hassle your wife.' " What mattered was, "Did they smack him around? Nope. Did they punch him in the face? Nope. Did they hit him with a telephone book in his testicles so that his testicles swell up not leaving a mark?"

Richman, who is uncommonly garrulous and delights in digression, claimed that this last treatment had been used on a client of his in upstate New York: "This guy, successfully, him and another guy raped and killed a girl. Then years and years later, seven years later, he'd turned his life around completely, and the other guy saw him, said, 'Look, we better get rid of the body.' They dug up the body and threw it over a bridge. The other guy gets arrested, rats himself out, then he gives up this guy. This guy now is a college graduate, has children, straightened his life out. Twelve years after the event, they call him in, he confesses—using that technique." Richman sounded more offended by the alleged abuse of his client than by his client's crime, but when he wound back to the question of Koehler, he could only say, "Nope . . . With this confession I didn't think we had a shot."

Of course, that's not what Richman told the prosecutors when they initiated plea-bargaining negotiations in the spring of 1998, nearly nine months after Koehler's arrest. Koehler had been charged with two counts of homicide and one count of criminal possession of a deadly weapon—the gun he was carrying at Penn Station. If he went to trial and was found guilty, he faced a sentence of fifty to a hundred years in prison for the murders alone. Saracco and Bibb, however, offered to reduce the homicide charges to manslaughter and said they would settle for a sentence of twelve and a half to twenty-five years. Richman said: Forget it. And so began the slow process of bluff that allows both sides to avoid going to trial by pretending that they wouldn't mind if they did.

"The secret in this phase is you don't give a shit," Richman told me. "You don't care and you convey the fact that you don't care." After all, he said, "I love court. It's a playground for me. It's an opportunity to show off, and I'm a show-off, you know."

CHAPTER ELEVEN

EVERY FEW MINUTES during my time with Murray Richman at his office, our discussion of the Koehler case was interrupted by a phone call or by a colleague or a client who strolled in to discuss a case or swap gossip. It wasn't unusual for these breaks to last longer than the patches of conversation we squeezed in between them. And although Richman occasionally signaled for me to turn off my tape recorder, for the most part he seemed pleased, even eager, for me to witness and record the antic theatricality of his peculiar moral universe.

[*Enter Stacey, his daughter, who works with him as an attorney, and Renie Arias, his office manager since the mid-1960s.*]

RICHMAN: What's the charge?

STACEY: It's rape.

RICHMAN: Fine. Call and find how much money is gonna be in the case—if it's a sure thing or not.

RENIE: What happened is he was in the room with the girl at her parents' house. He jumped out the window and broke his legs. He's in the hospital.

STACEY: He jumped out from the third floor.

RENIE: But that's not what the lawsuit is—he's got another pending lawsuit.

STACEY: Because the father tried to shoot him.

[*Enter Renie with a phone message about a narcotics case.*]

RICHMAN: Two Hasidic kids got arrested for Ecstasy, in France. Kids from Brooklyn. Seventy-eight thousand pills. Importation. They brought it—they were just couriers—from Holland to France to New York. At the airport they got arrested. It's a couple. A woman and a man. Twenty-one-year-old girl and a twenty-one-year-old boy. Newlyweds.

[*Enter Marco, an elderly Italian American client who is under house arrest and required to wear an electronic tracking bracelet on his ankle. A few months ago, his foot swelled up, he went to the hospital, and the doctors took the bracelet off. Now his probation officer says those months won't count against his sentence. He walks awkwardly, with a shirt tied loosely around his waist in an attempt to hide that he has soiled his chinos.*]

MARCO: I dirtied on my pants. It always happens, but—

RICHMAN: Marco, go home, get outta here . . . I'll get you the time—credit for the time . . . As sick as you are, you came in? What are you crazy?

MARCO: Aw, I got nervous. It's two months, two and a half months. My damn life won't last two and a half months.

RICHMAN: Marco, as long as I've known you, you haven't got that life to live. Remember thirty years ago? Your heart wouldn't make it till you're fifty years old.

MARCO: Thanks, Murray . . . Take care of yourself, buddy. I owe you dinner.

This was Richman at work. He appeared to be having a wonderful time, rocking and swiveling in his big executive chair and talking around a fat Havana cigar—a stout man, with an imposing paunch under an expensive necktie and a pair of suspenders embroidered with little blindfolded figures of Justice holding her scales.

[*Enter Joey, a lawyer on Richman's staff.*]

JOEY: You know what? There's only one trouble with the Mets.

RICHMAN: They can't do anything.

JOEY: But I'm serious. You know what it is? The fucking manager. Let me tell you why.

RICHMAN: Oh, stop it, Joey. God, listen to me. Piazza's not hitting.

JOEY: No.

RICHMAN: Toca's not hitting.

JOEY: No.

RICHMAN: Olerud's not hitting.

JOEY: No. That's true. But listen to me.

RICHMAN: That's true! That's the whole lineup.

JOEY: I mean. All right. Piazza's got a bad hand. Ventura has got a busted-up shoulder. You know. But the point I'm making is, just to give you an insight, this is supposed to be a team game. Now, Cookie Rojas got thrown out of the game. Right? Can't play for five years. You know, he can't manage, coach, whatever. Now, what do you want to do? You want to get the fucking umpires mad at you some more? Of course not. So what does he do? He hangs Rojas's uniform facing out toward the umpires. So they say, That's very fuckin' smart, Mr. Valentine—you see that outside corner that Maddux is getting? He's gonna get a little more now.

RICHMAN: Ohhh, the game's not that way.

JOEY: You don't think so?

RICHMAN: No.

JOEY: Murray, the whole world . . .

RICHMAN: Joey, you got the conspiratorial view of society . . . Don't break my heart.

JOEY: Look . . . Get rid of that manager.

RICHMAN: I don't give a shit.

[*Enter Rocco, a burly man with a voice like a cement mixer.*]

RICHMAN: Your father and I grew up together . . . Your mother is a beautiful lady.

ROCCO: She sure is . . .

RICHMAN: Your uncle—the first time I had him, he was thirteen years old.

ROCCO: Yup.

RICHMAN: I represented Nicole when she killed her mother, when she cut her mother's throat.

ROCCO: Yes, yes, I remember that.

RICHMAN: Your aunt winced at me. She said, "How could you represent her?" I said, "Well, I represented you, what was wrong with that?" She said, "That terrible girl, she killed my sister."

ROCCO [*laughing*]: I know that. I know . . .

RICHMAN: She did *one* year.

ROCCO [*still laughing*]: That's it, Murray. You know the old saying, Don't Worry Murray.

RICHMAN: Isn't that funny?

[*Enter Charlie, a hulking young Albanian American, wearing unlaced Timberland boots, baggy jeans, an open-necked sport shirt, and a fair weight of gold chains around his neck. He hands Murray a check for ten thousand dollars.*]

RICHMAN: Ahhh—love it—I love it when you bring my money. Makes me very happy. My favorite commodity. In any event, we got a couple weeks yet. We're gonna go to appellate with the gun. I'm gonna win the gun case. And we'll deal with the murder case after.

Once, when Richman's daughter Stacey popped in, he told her that I was interested in Koehler, and she said, "He's absolutely charming . . . He is really a nice man, notwithstanding the murder. But murderers are people, too."

"They need love also," Richman said.

"They do," Stacey said.

"Yeah." Richman chuckled. Then he said, "Murder's my favorite. I love murder. Always one less witness to worry about."

When we were alone again, he said, "Let me tell you, crime is so immature. You know the one thing I like about criminals over so-called straight people? There's a certain simplicity in most of their lives that does not exist in the rest of the population. I find criminals, even the fraudulent guys, are more honest than the straight people. They know they're bad people and they're doing bad things, but they don't feel lying is an appropriate thing to do. They'll say, I didn't do it, but, you know, there is a certain degree of lack of sophistication with relation to it. My criminals tell me they're lying to me. I know they know it, I know it, there's a simplicity about it, a simplicity. And there's simplicity about Frank, simplicity about Frank at all times. And I've always been impressed with that simplicity. By and large, murderers are the straightest guys in the world. Murderers are great, great clients. They've done the ultimate crime, I suppose, and everything else doesn't really trouble them."

Richman went on: "I don't buy this concept of the so-
ciopathic personality, the person that has no sensitivity,
no feeling, cold-blooded, the cold-blooded killer. I never
met a cold-blooded killer. I just had a guy in here today,
very tough kid. Anybody'll say, He's a stone, stone-bad
guy. Stone. He comes in and kisses me, so humble. I
mean, literally, a humble kid. The two don't fit together.
These are people that—everybody's a diamond. There're
so many facets. It depends on what angle you come at the
person from."

Richman's angle was fundamentally romantic. As a
young man in the early 1960s, before he was admitted to
the bar, he had worked for five years as a social worker
with Hispanic street gangs in his old neighborhood in the
South Bronx, and he still fancied himself a champion of
the excluded, the abused, the misunderstood, and the
misguided. "I'm ready to recognize that nobody's per-
fect," he said. "I'm ready to recognize that people make
mistakes. I'm not a bleeding-heart liberal by a long shot,
but I do believe that everybody has to be given the bene-
fit of the doubt." Prosecutors, he said, may think they are
doing "God's work." Richman did not enjoy such faith,
but he saw himself as performing a public service. After

all, he could do nothing for his clients except fight for their rights under the Constitution. And what kind of society would we have if that fight wasn't fought?

"Trust the authorities?" he said at one point. "Not at all." But then he went further and said, "Do I see a difference between the authorities and gangsters? Yeah, the gangsters are more compassionate." It wasn't clear if Richman entirely believed this; it seemed that he wanted to, but at the same time he complained, "The criminals you have today have no color." In the 1960s and 1970s he had admired the Mafia, with its seemingly strict codes of conduct and honor. But later, as he watched the top New York crime families unravel, betrayed by informers and undermined by what he perceived as a decadent new generation who made a mockery of the outlaw ethic they were heir to, Richman had become at first disgusted and then disillusioned.

"Years ago," he told me, "I made a comment to another lawyer who had said, 'What happened to all the wise guys?' I said to him, 'We're the wise guys. We bought into all that shit. We bought the *omertà* and all the other stuff and tried to emulate that bullshit. And it's all bullshit. Never was anything. We're the ones that kept

the standard. We kept the standard going as lawyers.' "
As for the mob, he said, "A lot of these guys today—I
can't understand how they got their button. How the fuck
did they get their button?"

But Frankie Koehler had restored some of Richman's
faith in the old gangster legend. "Frankie's black-and-
white," he said. "Everybody else is various shades of
color. You understand what I mean by that?"

"Like a movie, black-and-white?" I said.

"Exactly," Richman told me. "He's black-and-white.
You could see him in *Naked City* with Paul Burke and
Horace McMahon. You could see him there. You don't
see him in *Law and Order*. There's none of the subtleties
of *Law and Order* about Frank. There's emotion, passion.
There's none of that today." Today, he said, the pictures
are in color, but "the color is actually colorless," just like
the criminals. "When you saw things in black and
white," he said, "you saw the contrast, it made the neces-
sary impression"—and that was the quality he treasured
in Koehler.

In the course of the plea-bargaining negotiations,
Andy Rosenzweig paid Koehler several visits in jail
to see if there were any more unsolved crimes he knew

of that he might like to talk about. "Any homicides?" Rosenzweig asked at one point, and he told me that Koehler said, "I could give you about seven or eight, but I won't." Rosenzweig felt he understood Koehler well enough by then to know that he wouldn't give anyone else up. So he took it that Koehler must be referring to murders he had committed himself. The old D-D-Fives from the case files certainly suggested that Koehler had periodically visited New York from California, and Rosenzweig was left to surmise that he may have worked on those trips as a contract killer. But it was only a surmise. Richman, who praised Rosenzweig as "the straightest, most honest, most upright cop I ever met," sounded even more approving of Koehler when he said of his client: "He was smart enough to know to keep his mouth shut."

Rosenzweig had been hoping that the hint of compassion he had perceived in Koehler's expression when he mentioned McGinn's fatherless children might signal a deeper regret that could be harnessed to make him cooperative. But Richman wasn't particularly concerned about Koehler's sense of right and wrong; what he found appealing about the murderer was his capacity for strong emotion. "He's a person that feels deeply. He's a sucker for feelings," Richman said. As he saw it, Koehler had lost the will to fight at Penn Station because he felt abandoned and heartbroken. Koehler had been convinced that those nearest and dearest to him had ratted on him; he'd left his wife, who had always been loyal to him, and his girlfriend had given him up—"left him bad ugly," Richman said, adding, "I think he wanted to get caught. But he'll never own up to it. I don't think it's an intellectual thought process. I think that he just had nowhere to go, and jail was as good a place as any. You know, he'd felt comfortable there in the old days. He met some good people there."

AS I LISTENED TO RICHMAN expound on crime and punishment, I wondered whether he ever had qualms about the fact that in helping violent people beat a rap he might be helping them to go out and do more harm. "I've had such experiences," he said. "But I'll be candid with you. I've always been very callous. People have asked me, How can you represent people like this? I hate that question. It's obviously an ignorant person who asks me that question. Because it's an obligation, it's my duty, and I do believe in this Constitution, and I really buy that shit. I really buy the whole bag of works. I believe in truth, I believe in justice, and I believe that truth and justice will inevitably prevail. My version of truth and justice may be somewhat different from yours and somewhat askew. I'm not going to deny that. But I'm a believer in the system."

At the same time, he said, "If I defended only innocent people, I'd go hungry," and he added, "This business is a bullshit business anyway." He said, "To know the law is good. But to know how to apply it, to know your angles, is even better. It's a psychological game as well as anything else. Is it for real? I don't know. We're dealing with real people, with real lives and real unhappiness. And it's like a game. Everybody's playing their hand."

When he spoke in this way, Richman's pragmatic cynicism was tempered by a mood of quasi-mystical existentialism; his eyes widened, and his voice softened, taking on a confiding tone, as he pursued the notion that there is no solid, objective reality—only interpretation. Richman, whose favorite book is Camus's *The Fall*, told me that his father always said that life is a dream and he shares that belief. "What *is* is what you make of it," he said, and, "The past doesn't exist, there's only how we remember it." He is especially fond of reciting the words "The truth is that there is no truth." Richman attributed this last aphorism to Isaac Bashevis Singer. When I asked for the reference, he expressed astonishment that I was ignorant of Singer's story "A Crown of Feathers," which he then told, at length and entrancingly. But when he got to the words in question, they turned out to be spoken not by Singer, in an authorial voice, but by the Devil.

In seeking a plea-bargain deal for Koehler, Richman declared from the start that his goal was a sentence of no more than five to ten years in jail. "It's a little more than what he'd get for the gun, and he ain't doing his hundred for the murder," he explained, and he recited his terms like a mantra: "Five to ten. Always five to ten." The months dragged on. Saracco and Bibb slashed their original offer of twelve and a half to twenty-five and proposed a compromise settlement of seven and a half to fifteen. Richman said, No, and began making the motions to go to trial.

For his part, Koehler thought that five years in jail, followed by life parole in California, should be sufficient. "I'm not this bad guy they think I am," he wrote to his lawyer from his cell in the city jail at Rikers Island. "I never robbed or hurt any old people. I never raped or beat a woman. I never hurt a child. I don't deal drugs. I don't use drugs. I'm not a good guy, but to some I was."

But to live outside the law you must be honest,
I know you always said that you agree.

BOB DYLAN
"ABSOLUTELY SWEET MARIE"

CHAPTER TWELVE

KOEHLER WAS BIDING his time at Rikers Island, reading the Bible and *Thus Spake Zarathustra* and writing the story of his life in letters to his lawyer. He called this exercise in the memoir a "sort of fun therapy," and during his most frenzied epistolary period at Rikers he would write for as much as six hours a night, when "most everyone is asleep or too cold to talk . . . so it's my time, I can think, write and smoke." Koehler had dropped out of school after the sixth grade and did not read a book until the age of seventeen, when he was in the solitary "box" at the Elmira Reformatory and a guard tossed him a copy of *Oliver Twist*. But he wrote in a neat hand, with a voice as direct as his speech, and his prose had a natural ease, graced at times by an uncanny insightfulness that can only come from a writer's conviction that he has something worth saying to say. Koehler felt that he had come to the end of his run, and in one letter he tells Richman, "I keep going back in my mind to my childhood. It floods back with memories, good and bad. What's so funny is that even the bad seems good now. The reason, I guess, is that there is a future in the past, if only in one's mind, and with age—seventy coming up—and being locked away in the Tombs, I find very little future in my thoughts."

Koehler begins his reckoning with his birth at the beginning of the Great Depression. His parents were teenagers. His father was in and out of jail; his mother was hard-pressed to cope; and by the time little Frankie was three, he had been sent to live with an aunt in the solidly middle-class Richmond Hill section of Queens. There he enjoyed a level of comfort that left him unprepared for his return, when he was seven, to his mother's

care and to the tenement streets of Chelsea and Hell's
Kitchen. "I was getting my ass kicked a lot for a while,"
he writes of his abrupt encounter with this hard world.
"But I had a good teacher, my mother. She knew more
about mayhem than most tough guys in the neighborhood." She tossed him coins to encourage him to fight
and beat him herself when the spirit moved her. Within a
year, he recalls, "Most everyone walked real soft around
me. To help build my tough guy façade, I learned early on
not to show my fear and always make the first move."

School does not figure in Koehler's account of his
boyhood. The neighborhood is everything, and he evokes
the West Side of the late 1930s and early 1940s with
spirit:

We lived in cold water flats. No hot water in the
bathroom, no tub, toilet in the hallway a pull
chain. Six flights up. Rats, roaches, you name it
we had it. But we had fun, just the wrong kind.
Most of the people who lived around there
worked on the docks. The big shots were the mob
guys who ran the piers. Most of them were Irish
and everyone knew them. No one got out of line

with them. That's who I wanted to be, and years later, I would meet most of them, have a drink with them as an equal. My boyhood dream of the James Cagney movie would come true.

Jimmy Cagney was Koehler's passion, and Koehler watched his gangster movies as if they were documentaries. At the age of nine, he embraced Cagney's strutting, smart-mouthed screen persona as his ideal—"the thing I always wanted to be"—and as an old man in prison, he yearned for him still. One night at Rikers, Koehler wrote a poem, recalling how, as a child,

> *He would sit for hours in the RKO*
> *Watching Jimmy in all his glow*
> *Being the gangster he longed for so.*
> *He could hardly wait till he would grow*
> *To drive the fast car and count the dough*
> *With beautiful women all in tow.*
> *He showed them all, they all would know,*
> *When he got his gun he'd shoot them low,*
> *Or scare them all, then let them go,*
> *These dirty rats, who beat and hurt him so.*

Elsewhere Koehler writes, "I see the young kid who was me almost as a stranger, I don't know him," but in his poem he says:

> *This nine year old*
> *I had forgotten so long ago,*
> *He comes to me,*
> *To the cell that I must go.*
> *He comes at times of the ebb and flow*
> *Driving me crazy with questions*
> *That Solomon might blow.*
> *The little waif won't let me go.*
> *Hey Frankie boy, Where did Jimmy go?*
> *and*
> *How come life didn't turn out like a movie show?*
> *They changed the script in every scene you know.*
> *I just didn't have enough to play them all solo.*

Koehler was the eldest of five children, and in a "true story," written to Richman, he recalled a night when he was ten years old; his father was in jail on a six-year bit, his mother was out, and a figure appeared in the yard outside the family's ground-floor apartment. "The monster,"

Koehler calls him: "He looked ten feet tall and he was black, all the things we learned to fear." Koehler told his brother to fetch his mother's kitchen knives, which were "sharp and big," and he writes, "My battle plan was for us to stay close to me in the middle, my brother on the left and sister on the right. I would stab in the front and they would stab from the side." Waiting in the dark, knives in hand, the children watched the prowling figure attempt to force his way into their apartment: "He moved from one side to the other and the windows were all locked. We moved with him. When he could not get in, he seemed agitated and mean looking. My sister kept saying, 'Come on, you nigger.' She cursed him with every curse she ever heard in the house or on the street. We danced from one side to the other. I do not know what made him leave." If the man had got in, Koehler says, "I know in fear I would have tried to stab him." But looking back, he seems to identify as much with "that poor guy" who'd terrified him: "I wonder if he ever sat in the Tombs like me, and what story did he have, and did he ever tell it." Koehler titled his own story of that night "The Dance of Death." He concludes it by noting that two of his three sisters and his mother have since died, and he says, "We danced the dance young . . . and all that is left now is the dance."

Koehler was eleven when his father came home from prison: "The sun was out, my sister and myself were out-side, waiting for him, and he patted me on the head when we asked if he was him." But he remembers little more about the man, because within a year of his return, the father took sick, and six months later he was dead, at the age of thirty-two. "I don't even know if I liked him," Koehler writes. In fact, he says, "I can't, for the life of me, think of too many adults that were okay. The guy my mother went out with when my father was in jail was a nice guy. Any that were good went in and out of my life fast, so I grew up real resentful of people."

Koehler began stealing in a small way as a small child, and after his father's death, as he drifted away from home, he started "upgrading" his crimes, "breaking into stores, robbing cars and just running the streets." Even in memory, Koehler seems impressed by his early delin-quency. He writes of helping a friend beat up his father, because the man battered his wife, of stealing continu-ously—"anything we could find"—and he sums up, "I was not a happy kid, bad kid no, bad no, dangerous yes."

Still, he says, "I think if I had never seen a gun, things might have been okay." When he recalls shooting Billy Burns, he declares, "To say I've always been sorry is not, or never could be, enough," but apparently he feels as sorry for himself as he does for Burns, because he is quick to add, "Two kids died that day." Still, within forty-eight hours of his release from the Elmira Reformatory, he had embarked on the armed-robbery spree that eventually landed him in Green Haven Prison. And in 1962, when he was paroled, he entered "the world of big time crime."

At first, he says, "I stole freight, and quite a bit. That is, trucking outfits were my mainstay." Then, with time, Koehler got connected at the Coliseum, where a murderous feud between organized-crime factions had created a power vacuum that presented him with an opportunity: "They didn't see the gold mine in the building, only the big stuff, like who would write the insurance for the union, a few dummies on the books, companies to handle freight and stuff like that. But the guy who was taking book was not with anyone, no card game was cut, no crap games, no shylock, numbers wide open, and everything." Koehler and a partner arranged to preside over all those operations. He was the enforcer, "putting bull on whoever had to be bulled," while his partner answered to the bigger bosses, and suddenly, "Life was good, money rolled in, I moved to a nice place, my wife quit her job, and I was more or less on my way . . . I had friends who would do me favors and I would put men to work for them, help in any way I could. I was all over, uptown, downtown, Brooklyn and Queens. You name it, I was around. By 1966, I was flying high."

Koehler spent his take recklessly, betting on horses, seducing women, boozing at the Copacabana, P. J. Clarke's, and Toots Shor's, and mingling with many of "the major players of the sixties," including the mobsters who were portrayed in the movie *Goodfellas*. Yet even as he reveled in the excitement, Koehler claims, he grew disgusted with the life of crime. "I was turning into a piece of shit," he writes. "My ego got bigger each day and the phony in me went right along with it." Then people around him started getting bumped off by other people around him or by car bombs, and he says, "The song that set me off in those days was 'What's It All About, Alfie?' " Actually, the song is simply called "Alfie"; Burt Bacharach sings it, and it starts like this:

What's it all about, Alfie?
Is it just for the moment we live?
What's it all about when you sort it out, Alfie?
Are we meant to take more than we give,
or are we meant to be kind?
And if only fools are kind, Alfie,
then I guess it's wise to be cruel.
And if life belongs only to the strong, Alfie,
what will you lend on
an old golden rule?

"I sure couldn't get that answer," Koehler writes. "So it was have another drink, and back to this crazy life of silk suits, pinky rings, and bullshit."

Koehler's flight from New York to the West Coast in 1970 brought that life to an abrupt end. And at first he found small-town living in California difficult, especially the mornings, when he missed "sitting in a club, a drink in front of me, and talking to guys just like me or worse about other guys just like us, trying to get their piece of the pie, the cops you could buy and the bums you couldn't, the mob guys who were okay and the ones that were not, the big score that was waiting." But with time, he came to think of his new existence in tranquil Benicia as a kind of deliverance, "enjoying kids laughing, seeing families who loved each other, the good life." He believed he would never be found there, never have to run again, and he liked to imagine that if he had grown up in such a place, he "would have made it" as an honest, God-fearing "working stiff."

Instead, of course, he was sitting in prison, and the most striking thing about the tens of thousands of words he produced at Rikers is that he never acknowledges why he is there. Glennon? McGinn? Murder? Not a word. Koehler simply glides from New York to California, as if one day he had decided for the sheer goodness of it to renounce a way of life that was hurting him with its falseness and futility. In his telling, he does not shoot two men and take their lives; he saves himself and gives himself a new life. And judged by this measure, killing Glennon and McGinn *was* the best thing Koehler ever did.

WHEN HE ARRIVED at Rikers, Koehler was convinced that he had been "ratted out" by his nephew's wife in Benicia, and he says he pored over the Bible, seeking answers to his "pain and sorrow." But, he writes, "I found none, I cursed everything, I hated everything, most of all myself for being a fool. For months I felt sorry for myself. I wanted to die so bad . . . And then the thought would pop into my head, What if I die before I can get even? Day after day, this was all I thought of. There was no answer from God."

In fact, he says, "This is a place that God does not come. God is drugs, God is greed, God is dead in this world," and throughout his letters to Richman there runs a steady litany of complaints about the prison's "zoo"-like conditions. In a stray burst of rhyming prose, Koehler wonders, "How in the world could anyone imagine a place like this, where men scream tales of nothing just to prove they're alive and exist, if only to themselves, in cell block six?" He repeatedly fantasizes about committing suicide and at one point remarks, "At least the Chinese just shoot you in the head and get it over with. In my case, that could be a kindness." But he is more believable when he says, "All I want is a hot tub, some good food, and to be left alone." Still, Koehler kept grappling with spiritual matters in his prison writings, hungering for what he calls "a peace I can't define."

"I got a lot of stuff going on all the time, hot, cold,

love, hate, forgiveness and revenge, just no end to it," he tells Richman. "I sit every day, trying somehow to let go of my hate for people who have hurt me." And eventually, he reports, God did breach the walls of Rikers to speak to him, "the way he speaks to everyone," saying, "All things in life have been given you. Nothing good and bad have you not known. No one screwed it up but you."

Such reckoning does not sit easily with Koehler. Despite all his self-pity, self-evasion, self-indulgence, and self-deception, there is, as Richman would have it, a straightness and simplicity about him, at least where God is concerned, that render him incapable of pretending to a religious consolation that genuinely eludes him. "Religion, in any form, can't be the answer, but if you believe in something it's better than believing in nothing at all," he writes. Yet even when he hears God's voice, he is quick to remark, "I'm not a religious man, so I can't say I'm born again, or what's going on." And even as he flirts with humility, he sees himself as a universal figure: "If I can believe that Christ came down to save me, and all like me—which is everyone—then I may have a chance to get out of my hell, here and in the hereafter. I sure hope so, getting real tired of it all."

Time and again, Koehler throws his arms wide and rushes to embrace spiritual surrender, eager to receive its promise of forgiveness and redemption, and each time he steps back and knots his hands into fists. It's as if, as one who sees himself as both a taker and a giver of life, he can't stand the idea of a higher power. He simply refuses, as he would say, to "punk out" before the Lord. Yet in his stubborn resistance to letting himself off the hook of his doubts, he does not come across as an unbeliever so much as one who believes in the idea of God but cannot pretend to himself that he believes God exists.

As a child, Koehler had made communion and been confirmed in the Catholic Church; he had served as an altar boy and a choirboy; and despite his avowed agnosticism, he writes, "Religion was a big thing in my life, and I've always been glad for it. Over the years when I was going from bad to worse, I know it kept me from sins that would have cost my soul." He never says what those narrowly averted sins might have been, but he does finally turn back to the Bible at Rikers. And this time, he writes: "I ripped off my shield and, for the first time in my life, looked at myself with truth. No lies, no sad stories to hide this man, who had always done everything his way, wrong or right, without ever thinking of others first. Oh, did I weep, looking at it all. What revenge should I take on a man like this? Should I kill him? Should I let him rot?"

Koehler is much too fond of himself to continue for long in this vein. Almost at once, he finds himself thinking, "I'm not that bad. I've lived a crime-free life all these years, shouldn't I get something for that?" and then he writes: "What a laugh I had, the more I thought what a jerk I am. Who did I ever think I was, making deals with God?"

CHAPTER THIRTEEN

ON MAY 26, 1999, almost two years after Koehler's arrest at Penn Station and two months shy of his seventieth birthday, a small, blond woman in her mid-thirties with an attractive open face stood before the Supreme Court of the State of New York in Manhattan and said:

My name is Karen McGinn-Hagen. I am the youngest of Peter McGinn's four children. My father was only thirty-eight years old when he was

153

stolen from us, a young, handsome self-made businessman with a style and wit that my young brothers and sisters and I were just coming to know and appreciate. I was only six years old when Frank Koehler murdered my father. My brother Kevin was seven. My brother Peter was eleven. My sister, Maureen, was fourteen. Our young mother was forced, without her partner to help, to raise us. We missed and miss him very much.

Over the years we have worn out the pictures and the stories and the storytellers who have described our handsome and loving father, spending days and summers on the beach at Fire Island with his children. We remember him teaching us to ski and to ride horses. We remember afternoon baseball games and dinners at home when he tried his best to keep all four of us at the kitchen table. We miss him because of everything he was and everything he was meant to be. We missed him as children who sought his guidance. We miss him as adults who crave his counsel.

Today Peter McGinn would have been a grandfather of six beautiful children. He has missed it all. He has missed the first days of school, last days of school, two-wheel bicycles, driver's licenses, weddings, walking his daughters down the aisle. He has missed soccer games, college scholarships, and graduations. He has missed a lifetime of Christmases and Halloweens and Father's Days. He missed middle age. He missed retirement. He missed a chance to live his life. He missed a chance to grow old.

We stand here today, the grown children who waited our whole lives to see our father's murderer punished. Frank Koehler deserves to be punished for every hug, for every morning, for every time the sun shown on his face, for every time he celebrated, for every time he laughed, for every time he cried, for every minute, every day, every year that he lived and my father did not.

We, Peter McGinn's children, lost our father when a coward ended his life. It's our father's courage and strength that bring us here today to see Frank Koehler punished.

KOEHLER SAT a few yards away in his prison clothes. He had grown a scruffy white beard and was considerably thinner than he had been at the time of his arrest. When the presiding judge, Michael Obus, asked him if he had anything to say for himself, he rose and said, "My apologies are not enough to say to the families. I will probably die in prison. I will—probably, eventually. As a human being, I am sorry for what happened that night, not because I am standing here. That is all I can say."

Then Judge Obus explained that in view of the defendant's advanced age, and the difficulties that such an old case would present if it were to go to trial, the prosecution and the defense had reached an agreement in the matter of *The People* v. *Frank Koehler*. In accepting the deal, Koehler agreed to waive his right to appeal, making for "a final resolution of the case," albeit, Obus remarked, with a sentence that "obviously does not meet the seriousness of the underlying conduct of the defendant": for pleading guilty to two counts of manslaughter, four and a third to thirteen years in prison; and for pleading guilty to one count of criminal possession of a weapon, six and a half to thirteen years. So the gun rap drew a stiffer penalty than the murders, making it the "controlling sentence," and with credit for the time he had already served, Koehler will be eligible to apply for parole in the summer of 2003.

"Not too bad," Murray Richman said. He had stuck to his plea-bargaining position of a five- to ten-year sentence until the day before the case was supposed to go to trial. At that point, Steve Saracco and Dan Bibb had made a "final offer" of seven and a half to fifteen; Richman said, "No way, six to twelve"; and they agreed to split the difference. "Old-fashioned expression—we Jewed 'em down," Richman told me, adding, "Frankie may see the streets. I'm betting he does."

Koehler was not so sanguine. "Probably, if I was thirty years old, I'd be laughing, and if I was the same guy I was at thirty, I'd say, Wow, I beat this case," he told me when I visited him a few months later at the Gowanda Correctional Facility, south of Buffalo, where he was serving his time. "At seventy, it's a death sentence." He said his health was lousy—"I got high blood pressure, had a heart attack about five years ago, I'm still smoking, arthritis, the whole bit"—and he looked a little haggard in his beard and faded green coveralls, although he was hardly frail and his violence was far from spent. "I fight it every day," he said, smacking his fist into his palm. But perhaps he was right; perhaps he would die in jail. What of it? That didn't strike me as unfair, and I wondered whether he saw any justice in his finally having been held to account for his murders.

"Justice?" he said. "Justice for injustice." Then he said, "Is there a justice for taking a life? What would be just?" He couldn't think of an answer. But leaving justice aside for the moment, he said of his punishment, "It'll take my life. So, there you go. That fits the crime, don't it? And what have they got? They got a fucking body. That's all they got."

So Koehler regarded his captivity as a kind of legalized revenge killing, and he told me he wished he'd gone to trial and tried to beat the case. "You know why we didn't?" he said. "Because Mr. Andy Rosen-swagger there, who's a real smart fuck, he went to the priest."

The priest, it turned out, was Koehler's name for the good side of himself: the priest as opposed to the hoodlum, just like in the old movie *Angels with Dirty Faces*, which tells the story of two boys from Hell's Kitchen who get chased by cops for stealing some fountain pens; one gets away and becomes a priest, played by Pat O'Brien, the other gets caught, sent to reform school, and returns as a hoodlum, played by Jimmy Cagney. Although Koehler didn't mention the movie, he had internalized both lead roles, and when Rosenzweig had reminded him how painful a trial might be for those close to him, the two had struggled within him. "The hoodlum would've never went for it," he told me. "The hoodlum would've said, 'I don't give a fuck about the family, or anybody else.' But the priest in me, he said, 'That's bad shit, Frank, don't do that.' Very strange. There's a combination going on there." Koehler wasn't sure how that combination added up. "That priest is a dangerous guy," he said. "Or he's the best guy I got. One or the other."

Either way, he seemed to believe that the lashes of his own conscience were all the punishment he needed. "I beat myself to death pretty good," he told me. "My enemies don't have to worry, I do a good job." And where he failed, he figured God would sort it out. He recalled that one of the people he'd enjoyed meeting on the train to New York was a black woman from Detroit who'd lost her only son. Late one night in the smoking car, she told him "her troubles, her life," and said, "God never promised us nothing but death." Koehler heard many "interesting stories" during his final days of freedom and flight on the train, but he said, "That sticks in my mind."

He waved a hand around at the prison walls. "This is the terminal," he said. "This is where you argue all your life, what's right, what's wrong, what's good, what's bad, what's justice?" He glanced up at the ceiling. "Only the Big Guy's got them answers."

"You think he's up there?" I said.

"Jeez, I hope so," Koehler told me. "What a fucking waste it would be if he wasn't." Then after a moment, he said, "Or what a joke."

SHORTLY BEFORE I met Koehler at Gowanda, I spent a day in Benicia, California, following his footsteps up and down First Street. Everyone I spoke with who had known him there remembered him with great affection, and I heard one anecdote after another about how he would assist the sick, give food and shelter to the indigent, soothe the angry, and deliver stern and sound advice to restless and wayward youngsters in a manner that they heeded. To be sure, he had also been known on several occasions to dispense rough physical punishment to teenage vandals, but I met nobody who was not grateful to him for that, too. He was their unofficial mayor, and they missed him. After his arrest, a number of Benicians from diverse walks of life—an antiques dealer, a lawyer, a hot-dog seller, an artist, an ex-junkie—had written testimonial letters in support of his fine character; and for a time FREE NEW YORK FRANKIE T-shirts, emblazoned with an image of the Statue of Liberty, were sold and worn in the town. Even now, two years later, the prevalent attitude I encountered in Benicia was that Koehler had done his penance.

When I knocked on Koehler's wife's kitchen door, she told me, "I just want to be left alone from all this crap, I wish I could run away to another planet," but she invited me in. Across the kitchen window, a collection of the antique bottles Koehler had found along the bay shore was arrayed on shelves, glowing amber, blue, green, and frosty white. Beside them, a Rainbow Lory, a decadently colored bird from Papua New Guinea, scratched about in a cage. Koehler's wife was a stout, handsome woman in her mid-sixties with a youthful manner and a warm voice. As we sat down at the kitchen table, she touched her hair and said, "I wish I looked better—if I'd known you were coming." I told her I didn't have a camera, and she said,

"If you did, I'd turn the hose on you, like I did with the guy from the *New York Post* two years ago."

She watched me writing her words in my notebook, and she asked, "What good can this do him?" I said I hadn't come to Benicia worrying about what was good for Frankie Koehler. "You thought he was an animal," she said sadly. "Why? 'Cause he bit the bodies? You knew that? From the autopsy reports? His lawyer sent them out to me, and that made me sick. Just sickened me." She picked at a paper napkin on the kitchen table, and after a moment she said, "You want me to help you with this? Go back to when he was younger. He was given to an aunt. She couldn't read or write, and she lived with *her* aunt, who had all kinds of money. He was a Little Lord Fauntleroy, is that the expression?" Whatever he was, she told me, "You gotta understand about Frankie. He always felt unwanted."

Koehler's wife was just seventeen when she met Koehler, and he was just out of Elmira, so she knew from the get-go that he was a killer, but what she saw was "a frightened kid, really . . . so skinny, a pathetic kid," and she gave him her heart. "I was in love with a young boy and it never went away, because he has a lot of charisma, and everybody liked him who met him," she told me, adding, "You gotta understand how brainwashed women were in those days. I believed everything he said." And she still believed in Koehler: "It's like you hear all the time with people, and with him it's really true—if somebody had got him at the right age, and given him some guidance, he could have been a great man. He was smart, and fast, and he knew human nature. But one day, long ago, he gave a kid a good fight, and he was so afraid after that when he saw him again on the street. But then Frankie noticed the fear in this kid's eyes, and he became the bully, the big guy on the block."

She said, "What the hell did he know about anything? What did he know about the world?" She said, "He didn't know much, so he put a big act on. A lot of it was fear, and a lot was façade." She said, "You should ask him to tell you about the first time he had a real Caesar salad, and they cracked an egg in the thing." She said, "What did he know about women? Show broads? He got in with these guys with money who ran all around. But what did he know? Who was his hero? Jimmy

Cagney. He was living in an Irish neighborhood where they drink all the time and beat their wives. When he lived out here, he saw a different life. He'd never been fishing before. He'd never gone camping. He learned that out here." She said, "I wanted him to go to art school. I wanted him to go into acting. He could've been good at it." She said, "He's got a big ego. They all do. Men all do." She said, "I'm not making excuses for him." And she said, "You gotta understand. This is the man I've been with forty-nine years. Do you expect me to hate him? I don't really like him, the pain he's caused me, and the way he's treated me."

Koehler's wife knew that her marriage was hard to understand, but she'd been advised that if she got divorced, "they could drag me back and make me testify against Frankie," and as a practicing Catholic, she didn't believe in divorce anyway. "I made the vows on the altar, and it's not been easy," she said. "He knows I have to do what he wants." But in the end, she told me, "Actually, I was glad to get rid of him."

Koehler's ex-girlfriend Dolores remembered him more happily. I found her behind the cash register at

Leonard's Tot Shop—"Quality Products for the Personal Care of Your Children since 1949." She was an appealingly solid-looking woman, with big blond curls, wearing a green blazer and blue jeans and surrounded by all manner of cribs, high chairs, strollers, bassinets, baby clothes, teddy bears, bibs, and pregnancy paraphernalia, including a display rack of car cigarette-lighter adapters "For Breastpumping in a Motor Vehicle." Dolores had three children, the youngest of whom, a daughter, Koehler had helped her to raise, and she said that although he had been unable to have children with his wife, he had been a wonderfully loving father figure. She had left her first husband to be with him, and eighteen months after he returned east, she had remarried, but she said, "I loved him dearly. I could not love someone more."

Dolores was a devout Jehovah's Witness, a minister, in fact, when she met Koehler. "So if you want to go with the bad guy and the good girl, there it is," she told me. "But I was disfellowshipped. I told them I was living in sin with him." She allowed that there were "two sides in him," but, she said, "his kindness was more overt than his temper." She described Koehler as a man of many passions: he was a great reader of biography and history who "talked about Hitler and Napoleon, and all the things they did wrong, and could have corrected, because even Hitler was not all bad at first"; he also "talked about guns a lot"; he was "fanatic about cleanliness" and liked to tell a story about "how he once shined his shoes so much he shined a hole in them." And, Dolores said, "He was very paranoid. He liked locks. But I saw a very relaxed man that enjoyed life, and we were gonna be happily ever after." She called him "very spiritual," "very charismatic," "a very universal kind of personality," "not afraid of anyone," "hilarious," and "a great lover, oh, mmmm-hmmm." Of course, she said, "My husband is, too. I picked another winner. Because I really believe Frankie's a winner. He is a winner."

At the same time, Dolores told me, "He was always saying that only stupid people got caught. So actually he's stupid then." Dolores had known when she lived with Koehler that he was on the run and that he had been convicted for murder in his youth. But his past had never been quite real to her until the "very nice people" from the FBI came after him. "He was a character that was like a fictional character almost," she said, so being with him was "bigger than life, like you walked right into a novel," and "after that, all the novels were, like, passé."

"DELIRIOUS DOLORES," Koehler said when I told him I'd seen her. "I had the feeling that bitch was gonna give me up."

Then why, I wondered, didn't he get off the train before it reached New York?

"I wanted to believe," he told me.

"In her?" I said.

"Yeah," Koehler said. "I wanted to believe. Stupid."

For the first two days on the train, he had worn his gun in the waist of his pants, thinking, If something comes up, we'll hold court right here. Then he'd found himself in the observation car, watching his fellow passengers watching the landscape, and as he imagined them dying in a shoot-out, he said to himself, Jeez, what a legacy to leave, you fucking scumbag cocksucker. That was when he'd put the gun back in his suitcase. Another stupid move, he thought later, he should have left it on the train. "I could've got another gun in New York in a half an hour," he told me. "I could've got twenty guns. I could've got twenty guns, and a bulletproof vest, and hand grenades, if I wanted them."

Perhaps he could have. He told me that throughout his decades in California, he had dropped back into New York from time to time to see "old friends" and collect payments from them. "There was money coming to me that came to me," he said cryptically. And he also said that as he followed the treacherous feuds of his old underworld cronies from afar, "there was plenty of times I wanted to get on a plane and come back to New York and fucking blow away somebody."

So why had such a canny, well-connected, menacing fugitive made so many uncannily stupid moves? He hadn't even had the presence of mind to use a fresh alias when he bought his train ticket. It was as if he had grown so accustomed to having everything both ways—O'Grady and Koehler, priest and hoodlum, California and New York, wife and girlfriend—that he really had forgotten who he was, until Andy Rosenzweig and his men flushed him out from the cover of his double life and simultaneously forced and allowed him to bundle all his contradictory realities back into one inescapable self: Frankie Koehler, armed and dangerous.

Still, Koehler scoffed at Rosenzweig's suspicion that he had worked as a contract killer during his fugitive years. "I wouldn't kill anybody for money under any conditions," he said. "That's a scumbag does that." I asked him under what circumstances he would kill for free. "The logic in my mind?" he said. "Why would I kill somebody? I would kill them if they were endangering my family, they were endangering my friends, or they were endangering me."

"These two guys you killed weren't endangering you," I said.

"That's true," he said.

"Nor was the other guy that you killed."

"The kid?" he said. "I was a fucking baby, man."

I reminded Koehler that after he shot Billy Burns he had told Burns he deserved it. "Yeah, he deserved it," he said. "I figured he'd ripped us off." As for Glennon and McGinn, he told me, "They didn't deserve to get killed. All right? I'll admit to that." But he added, "I don't feel remorse for Glennon. I hate to talk bad about the dead, but that guy's name is like poison in my mind even now."

What was it about Glennon? Koehler's loathing for the man was the passion that had defined the latter half of his life, yet he still couldn't explain it, and I noticed that even Glennon's friends found it tricky to account for him. Charlie Connolly, a retired New York City police captain who had been close to Glennon and boxed with him in the Bronx in the 1950s, before they made the choices that put them on opposite sides of the law, remembered him as "a natural wise guy," and explained, "You could describe him as a Method actor. In some ways, he was always playing a role." In fact, Connolly told me, "Some of us thought Richie was the victim of his own hoax. Most people wouldn't bring an antagonist into a friend's apartment. When he brought this guy Koehler up to McGinn's, we thought he was probably being mischievous—you know, see if we can play with these two guys." Connolly, whose own father was murdered on a Bronx sidewalk—"mugged and beaten, left there to freeze, and they never caught the guys"—said he felt bad when Glennon was killed but wasn't surprised he'd been shot. "I think Richie was an enigma even to himself," he told me. "He was one of those people who are trying to be what they think other people think they are, and sometimes it's a bad model."

As I listened to Connolly, it struck me that Glennon sounded a lot like Koehler, albeit with an unloaded gun, and as I listened to Koehler when he called Glennon names—"a pimp," "pretty smart, pretty clever, pretty cute," an all-around "bad piece of work"—I had the same impression. Koehler reminded me that in the years before he killed Glennon, he had come to take a bleak view of his hoodlum existence. "The worst fucking shit world that God ever created on earth," he called it. "A garbage world, with garbage people. Very few of them lived the Jimmy Cagney ideal. The more I got into it, the more I seen it, the more I hated it, and the more I hated myself." He had grown so desperate and reckless that he was "a suicide case," he said. But for all his talk of taking his own life, his instinct was for murder, and I wondered whether Glennon had become a target for that instinct by presenting himself—in jest or in earnest—as a reflection of all that Koehler despised about himself.

"Maybe," Koehler said. "Yeah. Oh, yeah." Then, after a minute: "Actually, you know, what it was with me was my guilt."

"About your friend's wife?" I asked.

"That's what it was," he said. "When you get down to the nitty-gritty, it was my sense of guilt, my sense of not doing what you're supposed to." He had felt that his honor was at stake, and feeling that way he thought it was "ludicrous" to find Glennon, of all people, sitting in judgment over him. "If you're a guy that does everything by the numbers, I can listen to you, and you got a right to tell me I'm wrong," he explained. "But if you're a guy that does everything wrong, you've got no right to tell me shit. That's the way I felt about it, and I brought that to the table."

In the end, Koehler told me, killing Glennon and McGinn was both "a very sad fucking chapter" and "just one of them stupid things." But however you looked at it, he wondered, "What can you say if you do something real bad? Sorry? No, that don't cut it. I don't know what does. I can't bring them back. If I could I would. Even though I'm in here, I would bring them back—Aw, go fucking do whatever you do, you know. Even Glennon." He had to think about that for a moment. Then he said, "I wouldn't like it, but I'd bring him back."

CHAPTER FOURTEEN

ANDY ROSENZWEIG DIDN'T make it to court for Frankie
Koehler's sentencing. He had retired from the D.A.'s office twelve days earlier, and he and Mary had moved to
the Rhode Island shore, where they were busy preparing
for the opening of their new business—a bookstore in
Newport called Book 'Em. On Rosenzweig's last day at
the office, Tom Hallinan, the original detective on the
Koehler case, stopped by to see him and to watch Koehler's videotaped confession. "I thought it would bring clo-

sure," Hallinan told me later. "And it did, but it disgusted me. I came out of there, and I walked from lower Manhattan to Forty-second Street, because it disgusted me that a lowlife like this here killed those guys like you and I would step on a bug."

Rosenzweig, too, told me he had "mixed feelings" about the Koehler case. "What's funny is I got into it because I thought, I can't leave this thing open and unresolved, and I was thinking especially that I wanted to put it to rest for the victims' families and survivors. The thing I didn't think about was that many of them had long ago found their own ways of dealing with it. So while I was going for closure, I was just re-opening it for these people. My idea of laying it to rest was their idea of an upheaval."

That was certainly how Richie Glennon's girlfriend had reacted when several of Rosenzweig's investigators appeared at her door hours after Koehler was arrested. "I'd been comfortable thinking that he was dead, but I guess it just never ends," she recalled. "When they said he's still alive, I didn't believe it. At this point, my feeling was, I'm sort of over this, I'm through with my grief, and to bring it all up again—no, thank you." Seeing

Glennon dead all those years ago had made her realize "you don't know who's gonna come around and shoot you," and she had dreaded the prospect of taking the witness stand if the case went to trial. But, she told me, "I understood that Frankie Koehler didn't like being in prison, and I thought, Oh, isn't that tough? He'd just ruined a lot of people's lives for nothing."

Rosenzweig had never spoken directly with Pete McGinn's widow or children, and although his own bachelor party had been held at Channel Seven, he had only a faint memory of meeting McGinn. So he was startled, in the late fall of 1999, when a young woman walked into his bookstore and introduced herself as Karen McGinn-Hagen. She happened to be in Newport, and she wanted to thank him for catching her father's killer. They spent several hours together, and when I visited McGinn-Hagen later at her home in Connecticut, she told me that she had never known that the police had written Koehler off as dead in 1992. "You couldn't help thinking about my dad's murder without thinking the guy was out there and had never been caught," she said. "Then my brother was reading the *New York Post* on August 4, 1997, and he sees this headline, FUGITIVE NABBED AFTER TWENTY-SEVEN

YEARS, and he starts reading it, and he says, 'Oh my God, this is about Dad.' "

McGinn-Hagen had been fascinated to hear Rosenzweig tell the story of the investigation—from the moment he passed Glennon's old restaurant, The Flower Pot, to the arrest at Penn Station. "There were so many situations that were dead ends, so many times that he could have given up, and he didn't," she said. "That made me happy. He never once just put the case back on the shelf, even when it would have been so much easier than keeping going." In court, when she read her statement, she had made eye contact with Koehler. "He looked back, which I didn't expect," she said, "and it made me feel good that he heard what I was saying, and said something that showed he'd heard." And although she called the lightness of Koehler's sentence "horrible," she said, "There is comfort in knowing he may die in prison."

For nearly thirty years, McGinn-Hagen told me, her father's murderer had loomed in her imagination as someone "larger than life," a "terrifying" figure. "It's funny," she said, "it was almost like a disappointment—but such a relief—to see that he was just this little old man." Her older sister, Maureen, who stopped by during my visit, agreed. "I always wanted the guy's head on my wall," she said. "Then I saw him in court, and I thought, Him? He's just pathetic."

IT IS NOT Andy Rosenzweig's way to take thanks easily. Tell him he did something well, and he'll start brooding about all the ways that it could have been done better, and how if the world weren't so full of blundering and folly it shouldn't have needed doing at all. So Karen McGinn-Hagen's visit left him feeling "all churned up," and when she was gone, he began pestering himself with questions: Why—really why—did I do this case? Why now? Why not earlier? He didn't have answers. "Those questions were a constant for me before, during, and after the investigation," he said. And they exercised him especially in the months after Koehler's sentencing, because, although he had retired and settled (like Frankie Koehler) far from the city that formed him, in a quiet little hamlet by the water, he was waiting anxiously to learn whether a secret grand jury would hand down an indictment in the last big case he had presided over at the D.A.'s office.

Once again the case had been cold when Rosenzweig re-opened it, early in 1997. And once again the crime was murder. But this case had been treated—wrongly, in Rosenzweig's view—as a missing-persons case. On July 8, 1985, a New York plastic surgeon named Robert Bierenbaum reported that his wife, Gail Katz-Bierenbaum, had left their Upper East Side apartment thirty-six hours earlier, following a marital quarrel, and that she had never returned. Within a year, the case had wound up on Rosenzweig's desk at the D.A.'s office, but although he thought there was compelling evidence that Bierenbaum had murdered his wife and dumped her remains into the Atlantic from his private plane, they had never recovered a body, and there had been no prosecutorial support for seeking an indictment.

For eleven years, the case had been bothering Rosenzweig, and he couldn't say exactly why he had finally re-opened it, except that he felt it would be wrong for him to retire with it unresolved. It had distressed him to learn that Gail Katz-Bierenbaum's parents had both died in the intervening years, while Bierenbaum had moved to Las Vegas, then resettled in North Dakota, remarried, and fathered a daughter. What's more, there seemed to be a chance that a "surgically disarticulated" torso of a woman that had washed up on Staten Island might be linked to the case. So, as soon as Frankie Koehler was arrested, Rosenzweig assigned Tommy Pon to reinvestigate the Bierenbaum disappearance.

Throughout the summer and fall of 1999, as the case moved slowly through the grand-jury proceedings, Rosenzweig monitored its progress with nearly daily phone calls from Newport. And when he himself was called to testify, the main question that came at him was the familiar unanswerable: Why now—after so many years? "What could I tell them?" he said. "Just that I'm the slowest damn, most tiresomely methodical dot-the-i's-and-cross-the-t's investigator they'll ever meet." Finally, in December of that year, Robert Bierenbaum was indicted for murdering his wife. When he surrendered, the front page of the *Post* ran his photograph under the single word NABBED! Ten months later, when a jury found Bierenbaum guilty as charged, Rosenzweig expressed his satisfaction by asking me, "Now what am I going to worry about?"

NEW YORKERS WHO knew Rosenzweig during his thirty-three years as a cop and an investigator find it hard to

imagine him in retirement. "It's incongruous," Murray
Richman told me. "Andy? In a bookshop? Mr. Need-for-
Action? Weird." So I wasn't really surprised when, less
than six months after leaving the city, Rosenzweig told
me, "I've sort of got myself involved in an investigation
up here in Rhode Island—well, not sort of, I'm involved."
I wanted to hear more, but he said, "I'll tell you about it
some year."

I had telephoned him at the bookstore that day to
read him a letter I had just received from Frankie
Koehler, which said, in part:

> After you left good old Gowanda, I spent the rest
> of the day thinking about my life and yours. I was
> wondering what was your story. Could it be we
> are light years away from each other, or do people
> somehow have their souls in common? I never
> did find out how you view God, life, death. You
> asked me. I never got around to asking you . . .
>
> I hope no one gets hurt from anything you
> write—even the dead . . . I've hurt some of the
> ones who have loved me the most. On that score
> I've been less than a man. But somehow they for-

gave me and still stuck. Who knows why. That's a story—why would people still think good of this asshole?—that's a lot better story than cops and wops, as we used to say.

I spent a lifetime hating a world I never made, and people who had nothing to do with making it. Then I got a world that I could make and turned it into shit. That's a sin and a big one. What my fate should be, I must say I don't know. But if I could undo all the hurts I caused in this life for others, I would be happy to give my life. If all the dead could come back, then my life would have a meaning . . .

Tell Andy I tried to whack myself out with pills on the Island. They told me I needed twenty. I got thirteen together and I was being moved so I took them. All I got was sick and good sleep for two days. I had gotten a razor blade, but when I looked for it, it was gone. I figure if God wanted me dead, He at least would have left the blade.

"Yeah, right," Rosenzweig said. "Blame it on God." Then he said, "Hang on." I heard him put the phone down on a hard surface, and through it I heard him walk quickly away. A few seconds later, he was back. "Sorry," he said. "I just had to get the license plate of a car I saw passing. It's this case I'm working on. The crime happened twenty miles away, but you never know."

April 1999–November 2000